As In Heaven
So On Earth

*We sanctify Your name in the world
as they sanctify it on high . . .*

— *Kedusha (Siddur)*

As In Heaven So On Earth

*Practical Hashkafa
To Enhance Everyday Life*
— *Based On Chumash*

Volume 1

Rabbi Ezriel Tauber

written by
Yaakov Astor

ISBN Hardcover 1-878999-17-6
ISBN Softcover 1-878999-18-4

Copyright © 1995 by Shalheves.

All rights reserved. No part of this publication may be reproduced in any form or by any means, including photocopying, without the written permission of the copyright holder.

For a free catalog or direct sales (individual or wholesale), contact:
Shalheves
PO Box 361
Monsey, NY 10952
Phone: 914-356-3515
Fax: 914-425-2094

". . . her flashes are like the flashes of fire, the flame of the Eternal One (*Shalheves Kah*)."
Shir HaShirim 8:6

Printed in Israel

CONTENTS

Introduction: As In Heaven, So On Earth   11

Explaining the title of the book.
Why Study the Beginning? Derech Eretz Precedes Torah. Know Yourself. Burial, Boxing and the Search for Derech Eretz. No Derech Eretz, No Torah.

PART I
THE PURPOSE

1   Your Destiny   23

Explaining the root of unhappiness and finding meaning in life.
Happiness vs. Entertainment. The "Airplane". The Magic Word. Radiating Like Angels. No Moment is Meaningless. Sanctifying Everyday Life. The Power of Private Acts. A Moment Really is Priceless. The Most Crucial Challenge Today.

PART II
THE CREATOR

2   Reality And Illusion   63

Explaining the nature of reality.
The Film Projector and the Shadow. The Transformer. Ten Commandments, Ten Sayings. The Moshol and the Nimshol. Sabbath.

3   Coincidence?   74

Explaining the mystery of Divine Providence.
Is There Everyday Life? The Mystery of Divine Providence. Confessions of an Economist. He Did, Does, And Will Do. The Hidden Light. The Labor Pains of Faith.

4   Staying Connected   89

Explaining the symbolism of water.
Mikvah. A Definition of Holiness. Torah: The Real Mikvah. The Holy Ark. As the Waters Cover the Sea.

PART III
ADAM: PARTNER WITH THE DIVINE

5   The Divine Image — 101
Explaining the creation of Adam.
The Fifth Element. "Making" Versus "Creating". Different Orientations. Living up to the Standard. Partners vs. Employers. Adam's Choice.

6   Soul Mates — 114
Explaining the idea of marriage.
Givers and Recipients. The Maximum Desire. To Become One. The Woman's Curse and the Man's Curse: Helping Each Other Overcome.

7   And It Was Very Good — 125
Explaining the nature of sin and repentance.
The Twelve Hours. Teshuva. No Reason To Despair.

PART IV
PARADISE

8   Verse Of Transition — 135
Explaining the human contribution to creation (Genesis 2:4).
Hashem Elokim. For the Sake of Abraham.

9   The Essence Of Prayer — 140
Explaining prayer, selfishness, and G–d's pleasure (Genesis 2:5-6).
A World of Kindness. An Awakening From Below. Flipping the Switch. Working Out the Inner Person. Self-Centeredness. The Great Machinery of Heaven and Earth.

10   Soul Searching — 149
Explaining the idea of a soul (Genesis 2:7).
The Plane and the Pilot. The Tenth Saying. Citizenship. The Womb or the Tomb. Time Versus Eternity.

11   The Garden Of Eden — 159
Explaining the Garden of Eden as a symbol of living with joy.
Living Now. Every Moment has its Gem.

12   The Tree Of Life — 165
Explaining why Torah is called the Tree of Life.
Give Me Freedom or Give Me Death. Grabbing Diamonds. Choose Life!

PART V
CIVILIZATION UNFOLDS

13 Adam's Sin — 177

Explaining Adam's sin and the lessons for us from his failure.
Dismantling the Jigsaw Puzzle. The Evil Inclination. And the World Came Tumbling Down. Protection from Sin? Ochal Tochal. Duties of the Limbs, Duties of the Heart.

14 Garments Of Light, Garments Of Skin — 191

Explaining the "garments of skin" G–d garbed Adam in.
Clothing and Embarrassment. Busha, Levush, Teshuva. The History of the Garments. The Hunter's Garment. You Wear What You Are. A Robe of Majesty.

15 Cain And Abel — 197

Explaining the deeper implications of the first murder.
Cain. Hevel. Set-up for Murder. The Psychology of Blame. The Two Ideologies.

16 The Eve Of Disaster — 207

Explaining Noah's life and times before the Flood.
Noah's True Offspring. Noah and Abraham. The Sin that Sunk the Generation. Make an Ark.

17 After The Flood — 216

Explaining the events just after the Flood.
Permission to Eat Meat. Shem, Cham, Yefes: The Three Decision-Making Centers. Noah Debased Himself.

18 The Generation Of The Tower — 234

Explaining the implications of societal unity and disunity.
Final Redemption Missed. Making a Name for Themselves. Breaking Away.

Supplement A: 241
The Creation Of Elokim

Explaining why the seventy-two Jewish sages intentionally mistranslated the Torah when they were asked to translate it into Greek.

Supplement B: 243
The Twilight Zone

Explaining the events of twilight, the quality of twilight, and the power of being human.

The creation of this book
is in memory of our loved Zaida
Chaim Zvi ben **Shmuel Mayer**
14 Kislev 5754
28 November 1993

INTRODUCTION

As In Heaven, So On Earth

In the beginning G-d created the heaven and the earth." (Genesis 1:1)

"Heaven" in the opening verse of the Torah does not simply mean "sky." It includes all the spiritual creations as well: the soul, the angels, etc. "Earth," by contrast, includes everything which is material, temporary, and finite. Now, despite the fact that heavenly creations have obvious advantages over earthly ones the first verse is telling us that both "heaven *and earth*" are G-d's creation. As such they are *both* inherently as perfect as can be.

Despite this, the earth's perfection existed in a latent, unactualized state.

And the earth was chaotic and void, with darkness on the face of the deep... (Genesis 1:2)

❦ AS IN HEAVEN

The earth is a potential heaven. It is a veritable spiritual treasure chest brimming with heavenly possibilities. Yet, its potential is locked up and out of reach because it began chaotic, dark, and void. The greater plan behind this design *was to give humanity the opportunity to share in the process of unlocking the earth's spiritual potential and bringing it to full fruition.*[1] It would be the human purpose to fill the dark earthly void with heavenly substance — to bring order to the chaos and make earthly existence a mirror image of heavenly existence.

Adam, as we will explain (Chapter 13), not only failed to accomplish this but his sin sent the world into greater chaos. The earth became a gaping void, a cavernous hollow. It is now our job to fill this void and restore order — to make earth as heaven.

To illustrate, imagine two identical pictures — one a painting and the other a jigsaw puzzle of the painting. The painting — the non-jigsaw puzzle — is beautiful to behold, yet the viewer has no part in bringing it into existence. It is a finished product. He merely purchases it and hangs it on the wall. The jigsaw puzzle, on the other hand, is not limited to mere viewing. It can be dismantled and put back together. The one who completes it derives personal satisfaction — especially if it is a difficult puzzle which takes excruciatingly long to complete. He will feel a sense of pride over the puzzle that he will not feel from merely possessing the painting. He invested himself in the puzzle, and that makes all the difference in the world.

SO ON EARTH

So, too, life. G–d's creation included heaven and earth. Heaven is the painting. It is G–d's artistry and all a person can do is sit back and marvel at it. The earth is a "jigsaw puzzle." It is the same picture, but all mixed up. Adam's sin made everything even more chaotic. It was as if he tossed the jigsaw puzzle pieces in the box up into the air and scattered them to every corner of the room. He turned the earth into a place of deep emptiness, a place where G–d (and sometimes His justice) can seem to be hidden. The human task is to restore all "the pieces" to their original place and make the earthly picture a perfect reflection of the heavenly picture.

As in heaven, so on earth.

Why Study the Beginning?

The question is how — how do we know which pieces fit in which places? How are we to take our earthly lives and make them congruent to heavenly values? The answer is Torah.

Torah means "teaching," and the purpose of Torah is to "teach" us how to live in harmony with the Divine will. That is why there are 613 commandments. They tell us exactly how, in skeleton form at least, to make the jigsaw puzzle of our physical existence a unified reflection of heaven's artistry.

From this a question arises.[2] If the most important thing is to live a Torah life of 613 commandments, then why does the Torah begin with the account of creation, the

AS IN HEAVEN

Garden of Eden, the stories of Adam, Noah, Abraham, etc.? Interesting though these passages may be, is the Torah merely a history book? Does it actually matter whether or not we know what happened in the early days? If the 613 commandments are the most important thing, then why should the Torah be anything more than a straight-forward listing of them (something like the Ten Commandments)? In other words, what is the Book of *Beraishis* (Genesis) and its stories doing as part of the Torah?

Derech Eretz Precedes Torah

My mentor, Rabbi Michoel Ber Weissmandl, *zt'l,* offered a perspective. Our Sages teach: *"Derech eretz* precedes Torah"[3] to which Rabbi Weissmandl explained: If you do not have *derech eretz* (which we usually translate as acting nice or respectful) you cannot have Torah, no matter how much book knowledge you possess. In fact, if you do not have *derech eretz* you are likely to end up using Torah for negative, destructive purposes.

Rabbi Weissmandl then asked, "If *derech eretz* is a prerequisite to Torah, where did we get it from? Who taught us it to begin with?" Our *Avos,* our forefathers, he answered. They taught us the meaning of *derech eretz.*

And this is why Genesis is the first book of the Torah. Also known as the Torah of our *Avos,* the "Torah of our [Founding] Fathers" — it is the original *mesechta Derech Eretz* (full Talmudic tractate on what it means to have *derech eretz*). It contains relatively few actual commandments because its primary focus is to help us develop our basic Torah personality. By contrast, the *second* book of the Torah (Exodus) is where we first begin to learn about the majority of the commandments. Therefore, the Torah of our *Avos* (the Torah which teaches *derech eretz*) precedes the Torah of Moses (the Torah of 613 commandments) because *derech eretz* must precede Torah.

Know Yourself

What exactly is *derech eretz*? *Derech eretz* (literally, "the way of the land") is best translated as "respect" because it refers to something more than mere politeness, etiquette, superficial manners, or techniques to win friends and influence people. *Derech eretz* connotes dignity — treating others with dignity, and, even more importantly, treating yourself with dignity. If you do not treat yourself with dignity how can you treat others with dignity? The search for respect begins at home. And this is why self-respect is the essence of *derech eretz*.

What is self-respect? Knowing who you are. And who are you? You are a creation of G–d. He made you in His image. If you truly understand that you are made in the Divine Image can you fail to treat yourself with dignity? Can you fail to treat others with dignity?

Imagine a priceless treasure locked in an enormous safe which requires one million numbers to be set in order to open. Now, imagine turning 999,999 numbers correctly, but missing one number along the way. That one missing number prevents you from opening the safe. So, too, is each person a critical "number" in the divine scheme. Each human being was created for a specific reason; all have a special and unique function to fulfill in unlocking this great treasure and redeeming the world. If even one person fails to fulfill his assignment the entire treasure remains locked away. As Hillel taught: "If I will not do what I have to do, who will replace me?"[4]

Knowing that, how can you not love your neighbor? Even more so, how can you not love yourself? As Rabbi Akiva explained: "Love your neighbor *as yourself* — that is the great principle of the Torah."[5] You cannot truly love your neighbor if you do not first know what it means to love yourself.

The first point to keep in mind, then, is to respect yourself. If you have proper respect for yourself, then you will never belittle anyone else. Belittling others indicates that you have not yet discovered your own self-worth. You simply have not yet understood that you are made in the "image of G–d" (*tzelem Elokim*).

Burial, Boxing and the Search for Derech Eretz

The principle of respect for the human form goes so far that if you see a dead body — and it does not matter whether the dead body was Jewish or Gentile, rich or poor, president or peasant, saint or murderer — you must bury it. You may not leave a corpse unburied. Doing so is like putting the "image of G–d" to shame. This is also why Jewish law obligates Jewish soldiers to be as respectful as possible even with their enemies' corpses. Just because another human being was your enemy does not diminish the fact that he was made in the image of G–d. Once a human being is dead his body belongs to G–d, and therefore must be treated with dignity and put back into the ground from where G–d originally took it.[6]

We have to bear in mind that insensitivity for the innate divinity and dignity of the human form — the antithesis of *derech eretz* — runs very, very deep in today's general culture. Consider a boxing match, an event which regularly draws the attention of millions of viewers. Two men punch each other in the face until one of them falls unconscious. And the harder the punch the more the crowd cheers.

Can you imagine a saintly figure like the Chofetz Chaim attending a boxing match? He would faint at the thought. According to the Talmud, if someone merely slaps another in the face causing him embarrassment he is fined a great sum of money. Human dignity has been violated. The Divine Image has been violated. Yet, today, people punch each other in the face for fifteen rounds and it is a media event of international proportions.

Even "non-violent" sports feed into this ugliness. The craving for victory, for absolute dominance, underlies every competitive sport. Often it is not so much the victory itself which is cherished, but the fact that the loser has been embarrassed. There is an almost sadistic pleasure in fans cheering in wild jubilation when the visiting team has been humiliated, devastated, and vanquished. What are they so ecstatic about? The fact that a ball was put in a net? The fact that one team scored a couple of extra points? What is the inherent pleasure in that?

And this is not limited to sports. Consider politics. The mud-slinging and name-calling have reached new proportions in poor taste. A "good" campaign today is not won so much on how well one candidate presents his views, but on how many accusations, true or false, can be successfully mounted against the opponent.

The cause of all this is straight-forward: people have lost the meaning of human dignity. They have lost the real meaning of *derech eretz*. In the worst scenario they actively seek to denigrate the image of G–d. And we who live in the modern world — even observant, otherwise insular Jews — cannot help but to be influenced by this general trend. Therefore, **we must emphasize derech eretz today more so than ever before.**

No Derech Eretz, No Torah

Derech eretz precedes the Torah. If you want to be worthy of and benefit from the 613 commandments of the Torah you must first be living a life of *derech eretz*. If not, what religion, really, are you practicing? The essential lesson of the opening book of the Torah, the Torah of our *Avos*, is the lesson that you and I were made in the image of G–d. And only when we learn well this first lesson — the lesson of *derech eretz*: human dignity, self-dignity — can we truly be ready for what follows, namely the Torah of Moses.

Every detail, then, of every story in the Book of Genesis is vitally relevant for all Jews — especially today. The description of who the Creator is; how the world came into existence; how the Creator made the human being in His image; how human civilization developed (how people discovered G–d, as well as how they disobeyed and rebelled against G–d) etc. teach us how to develop the proper *derech eretz*. A careful study of the Book of Genesis, therefore, is one of the best things you can do for yourself *all year through*.

Part I

THE
PURPOSE

CHAPTER 1

Your Destiny

- *Explaining the root of unhappiness in today's world, the "airplane" we call life, the bottom line of Judaism, finding meaning in every situation, Hitler's real goal and how it was frustrated, the value of a moment, and the greatest challenge facing us today: insularity at work and home.*

The Jewish People are here today because long ago one man, Abraham, started asking questions. We, too, are here to ask questions. And the first question I would like to ask is: What is life? It sounds simple, but let me invite you to consider the following.

I am sure most of you celebrate birthdays. Can you explain the logic behind the celebration? What is the big fuss? You turned thirty, thirty-five, forty, forty-five, fifty. It's another year. You polluted the world some more. Can you explain logically — without any religion behind it — the rationale behind the celebration?

🍎 AS IN HEAVEN

Some people answer, "recognition." A birthday is a convention to recognize another year has passed. Fine. Imagine, however, the following: A man has just been sentenced to death. He is devastated, so the judge decides to console him. "Don't worry," he assures. "We will put you on a train that takes you to the electric chair, but along the way there will be eighty stations. And at every station you can make a party."

What will the guy do? Say, "Oh, thank you, your Honor, sir, you are so considerate?" Or yell and scream at the top of his lungs and resist until they have to drag him to the train? And once on the train, will he sit passively? Not likely. First, he will try to stop it. He won't be able to, though. Then, he will try to jump off. He won't be able to do that either, though. What will he do by the fortieth station? Make a party? Celebrate? Every station is one step closer to the electric chair!

It sounds funny, but this is our situation. The minute we were born we were sentenced to die. They put us on a train. This train picked us up in the hospital and will later deposit us at our grave. We try to stop the train. It doesn't stop. We try to jump off. We can't. Is it a consolation to say, "Don't worry, we have seventy, eighty, or ninety stations along the way to make a party"? One year has just died on us. We are never going to see it again. Why should we celebrate? Why should we make a party?

You want a convention, a form of recognition? How about this: Each year let us make a "mock" funeral! It may

SO ON EARTH

sound morbid, but at least it makes sense! The way we do it now, though, we suffer for eighty years and then finally, after it is too late to change, the Rabbi comes to eulogize us. We can't even jump out of the box to say anything back. If we would celebrate each passing year with a mock funeral, on the other hand, at least we could hear sixty or seventy eulogies! Maybe then we might improve something in ourselves.

I am speaking facetiously, but my aim is to get you to think. This is a very down-to-earth question. And it has nothing to do with religion. Why do we celebrate birthdays? (Once a woman in the audience answered, "The reason is because a birthday is really a sad day. We make a party to forget how sad it is." Her comment was only too true.) If you are like most people in the audiences I ask this question to you are probably unsuccessfully groping to find a satisfying answer.

Happiness Vs. Entertainment

Let me ask another question: All humanity, from the beginning of documented history until today, has commonly pursued one goal: happiness. Has it been accomplished? Are people really happy? Have you ever met a happy person? Are you happy?

When I ask this question to an audience I usually get no more than a hand or two. Then I say, "Now, I sincerely think you believe you are happy, but you probably do not know the definition of happiness." After I define real happiness I usually do not even get that hand or two.

The phenomenon that people are unhappy despite the fact that civilization has been in pursuit of happiness for thousands of years should be an eye-opening lesson for us. Most everything else civilized humanity has ever tried to attain has been attained: they dreamed about putting a man on the moon — they put a man on the moon. They wanted to cure disease — they developed modern medicine. They wanted greater comfort — they developed technology. The one thing not attained, however, is a happy society — and this despite the fact that since the beginning of civilization innumerable philosophers have philosophized about it; gurus, shamans, and psychiatrists have promised it; and politicians have made its pursuit an inalienable right.

I would go so far as to say that the primary drive behind all the modern scientific discoveries, especially those related to the entertainment field, is for one thing: a little happiness. And indeed over the past century science has made some unbelievable accomplishments. If 150 years ago someone told us that we would be able to watch a movie one day, would we believe him? Well, we got a black and white movie. And then we got one with sounds. And then with color. Yet, did it make us happy?

Next people said: "If I could only get a movie in my private house — Ahhh! that would be paradise. No more waiting on long lines, sitting in a dark room, etc."

SO ON EARTH

Well, we got movies in our private homes. Videos, cable TV, world-wide news — whatever we want to see we can get at home now at the touch of a finger.

And we are still not happy.

Why? Perhaps because it is too difficult to get off the Lazy Boy chair and turn the channel. "If I could only get a remote control button — Oh boy! then I would be happy."

Well, we got that, too, and still we are not happy.

(Whenever I travel to Israel and see Bedouins it never ceases to amaze me how they have absolutely nothing — they live in the most primitive conditions: in tents without water, electricity, or toilet facilities — yet, a portable TV, that they do have!)

Billions and billions of dollars — the number one industry in America is entertainment — and still people are not happy. To the contrary, people are more unhappy today than ever before. In fact, those who are the most dependent on entertainment are the most depressed people; they live the most unproductive lives.

What can we learn from this? When we look into it we will see that the reason civilization has never attained the ideal of a happy society is because it has not really had a definition of life! Lacking that definition it cannot possibly attain happiness; and that is why people so intensely pursue entertainment (read: distraction) instead. *Entertainment is really a way of running away from ourselves.* And the better they let us run away from ourselves — Ahhh! that's the best entertainment! When you can say about a weekend,

AS IN HEAVEN

"The weekend flew by without noticing it. Thank G–d, I forgot who I am" — that was a great weekend. In reality, *entertainment is a form of killing ourselves.* (Modern society has a phrase: "killing time," to which I once heard someone comment, "Killing time is not murder; it's suicide.") The bottom line is that what most people equate with happiness is in reality nothing more than the slow, painless process of suicide.

What am I driving at? *The least appreciated commodity — the least appreciated experience — is life!* We will do anything just to ignore life, to be busy with something else. Just to push and push the days. Again and again . . . until one day you find yourself — if you find yourself living that long — sitting in a wheelchair, in a nursing home, and then all you do is count the cars as they pass by your window, think about memories, and tell yourself, "Is this what life is all about?"

In my opinion, this is the greatest mistake people make: We will discuss philosophy — Jews in particular will discuss the Holocaust, the State of Israel, anti-Semitism, history, and Reform-Conservative-Orthodox issues — we will discuss everything and anything, except the most basic, fundamental question of all questions — WHAT IS LIFE? That question we totally ignore. Yet it is the foundation of everything. Without a definition of it, all our philosophizing is nothing but towers of ideas built on air.

SO ON EARTH

Why are we unhappy? Because we have not taken the time to study the topic which is life. And this is the first point we have to address before anything else.

By the way, I have lectured on this topic — which is the theme of our book *Choose Life!* — from North America to South America; from Russia to Europe; from Hong Kong to Bangkok; from Johannesburg to Jerusalem — with secular people and religious people; with the most successful and the most downtrodden; with intellectuals on college campuses and criminals in prisons; with the wealthiest and healthiest as well as the most poor and seriously ill. *It is one topic which speaks to everyone,* because everyone is guilty of the same thing: not knowing what life is, and not even taking time off from the business of running away from life to try to discover what it is about.

The "Airplane"

If we do not fully know the value of life we cannot be happy with it — no matter how many comforts and gadgets we surround ourselves with. On the other hand, once we comprehend the true value of life, then even difficulty and hardship do not detract from feeling great happiness and enthusiasm.

Imagine the following scenario: You buy property in Australia and the next day someone makes you an offer for ten million dollars more than you paid. In other words, you can literally make ten million dollars overnight! There is

AS IN HEAVEN

one catch, however. You have to personally be in Australia within the next day and a half or the deal is off.

Now, a flight to Australia from New York takes roughly twenty-five hours and there is only one flight out of Kennedy Airport. If you miss that flight you will never make it, so you rush to the airport, approach the ticket office, and say, "I need a ticket."

"Sorry, everything is sold out."

You look into hiring a private plane. There is no such thing.

What else is there for a desperate person to do but take $20,000 cash, go to the manager, put it down on the table and say, "Listen, I MUST be on that flight, no matter what! Put me in the bathroom. I don't care. But I must be on that plane."

The manager takes the money, calls the head steward and says, "Take this man, put him in the bathroom and shut up."

You are on the plane. And imagine a flight sitting in a bathroom for twenty-five hours. Every ten minutes you are chased out. People look at you and ask, "What is that guy doing here?" Imagine such an experience. That is passenger A.

On the same flight is passenger B. Passenger B is a multi-millionaire. Every day millions are coming into his bank account (after taxes) and he does not know how to get rid of it fast enough. But he is a miserable character. His wife just threw him out of his house. His family has

SO ON EARTH

disowned him. He feels no affection for anyone. And no one feels affection for him.

Then he gets an idea: "I need some affection and attention. Let me buy a ticket on a long-distance flight and get pampered for a few days." He buys a first class ticket, gets red-carpet service, and lets everyone know he has money to burn. For every glass of champagne he gives a $100 dollar bill for a tip. All the stewardesses buzz around him like bees. He is the most doted passenger in the world.

Now, imagine asking the following to the passengers on the plane: Who is the happiest passenger on this flight and who is the most miserable? Superficially, everyone would say the happiest one is the rich guy laughing it up in first class. And, who is the most miserable? The guy in the bathroom. What is the truth? The exact opposite. What makes the guy in the bathroom the happiest passenger and the guy in first class the most miserable?

. . . Destiny.

Where are you going? What is your destination? The guy in the bathroom is anxious to get there. He knows why he is on the plane. He is willing to make any sacrifice to be on the flight. The guy in first class, on the other hand, has no destination, no destiny. It does not matter how good the conditions are that he is temporarily enjoying — he is the most miserable person.

Ladies and gentlemen — we are all on this plane. Some of us fly seventy years, some eighty, some ninety. But we are all on a flight. And it is going to end one day.

AS IN HEAVEN

What do we do about it? We struggle to acquire a window seat, a center seat, an aisle seat; first class, second class, etc. — but none of that is going to make us happy. On the other hand, if we find out what our destiny is — why we are on the flight — that! will make us happy.

The Magic Word

A business has many divisions. There is a purchasing division. A selling division. A manufacturing division. Advertising. Employment. And so on. No matter which division of the business you are involved with, though, there is a magic word you must know if you want to be successful. That magic word is "money."

Business is driven by profit. A businessperson is in business to make money. That is the bottom line. If you remember that, then no matter which division you are involved with you will make money. If you are involved with the buying division you know you will have to buy cheap to make money. If you are in the selling division you know you will have to sell expensive in order to make money. Money is the magic word.

What is the magic word in Judaism?

Some of you are thinking: *Moshiach* (the Messiah); others are thinking *Shabbos* (to keep the Sabbath), to keep the Torah, to do *mitzvos* (commandments), to be a holy Jew, to be this, to be that, etc. That's all true. But those are only tools to accomplish an ultimate accomplishment. Just as in business "buying" and "selling" are tools to accomplish the

SO ON EARTH

bottom line, so, too, *Moshiach*, the Sabbath, the commandments, etc. are only tools to attain the "bottom line" of Judaism. What, though, is the bottom line?

The answer is *kiddush Hashem*, to sanctify G–d's name.

Kiddush Hashem

Yisgadal vayiskadash shmay rabbah . . . — "Glorified and sanctified be THE GREAT NAME . . ." (*Kaddish*)

Yakiru viyaidu coll yoshvai saival — "Let it be recognized and known among all the inhabitants of the world [that there is a G–d]." (*Alenu* prayer)

We are here to bring the world to the realization that *Hashem* (G–d) exists. Of course, this means more than merely eliciting the acknowledgment that G–d exists, but includes the awareness that one is *constantly* living in G–d's presence, and that one sees G–d in everything which transpires. (See Chapters 2 and 3.) Indeed, G–d's name can be constantly on our lips and near to our heart or very far. The cultivation of that awareness is in human hands. It is called *kiddush Hashem*.

The opposite of *kiddush Hashem* is *chillul Hashem*, a "desecration of G–d." The Zohar points out that the word *chillul* is related to *chalal*, a "hollow" or "vacuum." Whenever people fail to see or understand G–d, a hollow or void — a *chillul Hashem* — exists. Our mission is to fill[7] the hollow and make the world — the entire world — aware of His Presence.

❧ AS IN HEAVEN

Kiddush Hashem means acting in a way that is congruent to the heavenly order, and thereby making life on earth a reflection of heaven. As in heaven, so on earth. And all humanity is expected to act in this fashion. Among all humanity, though, only one entity is designated to lead the way: Israel, the Jewish People.[8]

"I, *Hashem*, call you in righteousness . . . to make you a light unto the nations." (Isaiah 42:6)

Nikdashti bisoch bnai Yisroel, "I will be sanctified in the midst of the Jewish People." (Rosh HaShannah and Yom Kippur prayers)

Israel is chosen to be the leader in the field of *kiddush Hashem*. *Kiddush Hashem*, therefore, is the "magic word" in the "business" of Judaism. It is the bottom line. And it is even more demanding than business. In business you work during the day and then go home to your private life. The business of Judaism is not so. A Jew is in the business of making *kiddush Hashem* twenty-four hours a day, seven days a week. And therefore we have a Torah which guides us twenty-four hours a day, seven days a week. When we follow the Torah and live a Torah life we bring the awareness of the existence of G–d into the world. This is called *kiddush Hashem*, sanctifying G–d's name.

SO ON EARTH

Radiating Like Angels

To illustrate, let me tell you the true story of a *gair tzedek*, a righteous convert, who lived in Nitra, Czechoslovakia before the Holocaust. He converted shortly after the First World War when it was an extremely difficult time for Jews. Nevertheless, he became a righteous convert and raised a beautiful, deeply religious family. In World War II, when the Nazis occupied Czechoslovakia and started deporting the Jews, the gentile family of this convert came to him and offered to save him.

"I am a Jew," he responded to them, "and I am going to share the fate of all my Jewish brothers. Whatever happens to them will happen to me."

He was eventually deported with the other Czechoslovakian Jews. And there were eye-witnesses who testified that when he was standing in line to the gas chambers he was singing and dancing, thanking G–d for the privilege of dying because he was Jewish!

How did he attain this level of commitment? What made him convert in the first place, when the living conditions of the Jews in Europe were so harsh? I heard the answer first hand from a man who asked him himself.

"One Yom Kippur night," the convert explained, "I passed by the Jewish synagogue in Nitra and saw all the people dressed in white. They looked like angels. Their faces were beaming and shining. There was an otherworldly radiance to them. Then I realized that they were the faces of the Jewish friends I had business dealings with during the year. I could hardly recognize them. 'If there exists such a religion,' I said to myself, 'which can transform simple, ordinary, working people into angels, then that religion is the one I want to belong to.' "

Our purpose here is to transform everyone who comes in contact with us (including ourselves) into vessels radiating the presence of G–d. After dealing with us they should want to say, "I wish to become like that." When we live up to the religious and ethical standards of Torah — *and when we do so radiating excitement, happiness, and holiness* — we transform the world. This is the power of *kiddush Hashem*, of living life knowing your purpose.

No Moment Is Meaningless

Let us return to the question we began with: Why are people unhappy? The answer is because they do not know what they are doing here. They do not know the purpose of life. And what is that purpose? To make *kiddush Hashem*. When we know our purpose, then even mundane activities can be meaningful.

The Talmud tells us, for instance, that G–d asks us to make one hundred blessings a day. Why? Because in every blessing we say, *Boruch atoh Hashem . . . MELECH haolam*, "Blessed are you, G–d . . . *KING* of the universe." And each time we say, "G–d, *KING* of the universe," we remind ourselves that He is our king. Acknowledging that G–d is our king is akin to making *kiddush Hashem*. It is a way of saying I acknowledge G–d's influence in my life. And in

SO ON EARTH

fact that is why G–d made us with a need to eat, to drink, to go to the bathroom, etc. — to say a blessing after each of these mundane, everyday activities.

When we know our purpose we can never be unhappy, since there is no situation in life which prevents us from performing a *kiddush Hashem*. Indeed, everything can be taken away from a person — wealth, health, marital harmony, loved ones, parents, teachers, etc. — except one thing: the opportunity to make *kiddush Hashem*. No tragedies, no sufferings, no Hitlers, and no Holocausts can take away our ability to sanctify the name of G–d. To the contrary, the more that is taken away the more opportunity there is to make *kiddush Hashem*.

In the concentration camps, for instance, Hitler took away everything: he took away the Sabbath; he took away the opportunity to eat *kosher* food; he took away family life — the one thing he could not take away, though, was the Jew's ability to make *kiddush Hashem*. When Yom Kippur came and a Jew ate some food to save his life (as the Torah commands him to do in that situation), and from that meal he was able to live a little longer so he could then secretly join nine other men to say *Yisgadal vayiskadash shmay rabbah* . . . — "Glorified and sanctified be THE GREAT NAME . . ." — could there be a greater *kiddush Hashem*?

Hitler did everything to desecrate the name of G–d, to prove that G–d is not G–d, that the Jewish People are not designated to be "a light unto the nations." His entire war against the Jewish People was not primarily physical. He

AS IN HEAVEN

wanted Jews to deny G–d. When G–d told us, "You should be a holy nation representing Me," Hitler said, "I am going to show you that you do not represent G–d. You are going to deny G–d. You are going to rebel against G–d. You are going to get angry at G–d."

What happened, however? Under circumstances where people had the opportunity to become the most angry at G–d Jews snuck away and said, *Yisgadal vayiskadash shmay rabbah.*

Sanctifying Everyday Life

Kiddush Hashem does not only entail literally giving up one's life, and it is not only for concentration camps. I often say that, today, it is not our challenge to die for *kiddush Hashem.* Today, we have to do something which is even harder: We have to live for *kiddush Hashem* — with our day-to-day hardships. Let me illustrate this with a true story.

A few years ago, a very educated woman — a European news correspondent — made a tour of America and came to one of my lectures. She approached me afterwards and said, "I am shattered. I can't believe what I have just heard. I am the daughter of a Holocaust survivor. My father came from Poland and was so angry at G–d that he went out of his way to raise my sister and I anti-religious. I have never heard anything positive about G–d or Judaism from him. Yet, here you are — a Holocaust survivor — and proud of it, sure that we have accomplished something by it."

SO ON EARTH

To make a long story short, the woman became fully Torah-observant. And her father became sick over it. "I went out of my way," he told her, "to throw away the religion and now you want to come back? Are you out of your mind? Do you know how much you are upsetting and embarrassing me?"

She came to me crying, "What should I do? He wants to disown me."

"Let me meet your father," I suggested.

"G–d forbid. He is so angry at you. You were the one who made me *meshuga*! he says. I'm afraid to let him in the same room as you." I had to back down and let the matter go.

Eventually, she decided to move to Israel. Some time afterward, I traveled to Israel myself to give a series of lectures. The woman came to see me one afternoon and told me the following. As it turned out her father had come to visit her and was staying at the very hotel I was supposed to lecture in that evening. When she saw a poster announcing my lecture she hurriedly arranged to see me.

"How is the situation with your father?" I asked.

"Still very bad," she said.

"Try bringing him to the lecture tonight. Maybe something will happen."

That night, as I spoke, I did not know if they were in the audience or not. The main theme of the lecture was *kiddush Hashem*: that our primary purpose is to sanctify the name of G–d. And there are two ways to sanctify G–d's name, I

AS IN HEAVEN

explained. One is to die for *kiddush Hashem*, and the other — in many ways harder — is to be willing to live for *kiddush Hashem*. To illustrate what I meant, I told the story about one of the ordeals Jews had to undergo in Treblinka.

Treblinka was one of the most brutal concentration camps. In less than a year they slaughtered some 850,000 Jews. And it was not enough for them to kill Jews. They tried to denigrate them, as well. One of their methods, for instance, was to take the synagogue curtains — the curtains which cover the ark where Torah scrolls are housed — and hang them over the entrance to the gas chamber. The wording on the curtains read: "This is the gate to G–d where the righteous walk through." Their intent was to get the Jew to spend the last moment of his life cursing G–d.

In actuality, however, it had the exact opposite effect. When even the most assimilated Jews saw this curtain inscribed with the words, "This is the gate to G–d," many of them woke up spiritually and even danced and sang as they entered the chambers! They realized that it truly was the gate to G–d they were entering.

That, I explained, is what is called dying for *kiddush Hashem* — a sanctification of G–d's name in death. However, there is another form of sanctifying G–d's name, I told the audience, which in many ways is much harder: it is the *kiddush Hashem* of living after the Holocaust. It is the *kiddush Hashem* of those who survived and quietly went about the business of rebuilding their lives, their families, their communities — until they were ready to build a new

SO ON EARTH

synagogue and put up new curtains on which they wrote: "This is the gate to G–d where the righteous walk through." That type of *kiddush Hashem* is at least every bit as great a sanctification of G–d's Name.

"All of us," I concluded the lecture, "are survivors of the Holocaust — the physical Holocaust and now the spiritual Holocaust. Our job is to make a *kiddush Hashem* where we are right now, no matter under what circumstances we find ourselves in."

After I finished, all of a sudden the woman ran up to me and said, "You know, my father is here tonight."

"Why not bring him up here now?" I suggested.

She then disappeared into the crowd and returned a few moments later, escorting her old father. His head was bent forward. His eyes were swollen with tears. There was a long moment of pause and then he said in Yiddish, "Rabbi Tauber, I want you to know that I was in Treblinka." His voice was cracking with emotion. "And I saw the crematoriums with those very curtains you spoke about tonight . . . ." He paused a long moment and then added, "That's what made me an *apikorus* (a non-believer). I was so angry at G–d. Why did You let me survive? I asked Him. I asked a million times: Why did I survive!? Why couldn't I have been killed with my family and loved ones!? Why did I have to go through hell and then have to live with it!? Are You so cruel that You had to torture me with a living death!? That is the pain I have been living

AS IN HEAVEN

with," he said. "And that is why I became anti-religious. I never got an answer to my questions."

"Didn't you get your answer tonight?" I replied. "Although you thought that you could fight G–d by rebuilding a secular family, nevertheless, your daughter found her way back. She is the one who is making those new curtains and inscribing on them: 'This is the gate to G–d.' When you see her isn't it clear that you were not punished with life? You were rewarded with life."

He could not hold back any longer and started crying. We made an appointment to meet shortly thereafter and spoke for two hours. Afterwards, his entire outlook changed. He accepted his daughter and made peace with G–d.

Similarly, many — many! — of us are holding on to so much pain. I don't know if I can give everyone the specific answer he or she needs, but one thing I know for sure: Each of us has a unique purpose for which we were created. No person is lost as long as there is life in his or her body. We are never bankrupt of the ability to make *kiddush Hashem*. And the reason is because the WHOLE purpose we are here is to make *kiddush Hashem*, no matter who we are or what we have experienced.

Knowing one's purpose does not ensure that life will always be rosy. Often in fact it entails great difficulty — but this is precisely the point. An easy life is not necessarily a successful or good life. A meaningful life is a life of *kiddush Hashem*, a life where the person finds within himself or herself the strength and courage to withstand short-term,

SO ON EARTH

seemingly negative discomforts for the sake of making *kiddush Hashem*. And whether it is now or later — whether it is apparent or not — every act of *kiddush Hashem* cuts across time and space to produce monumental after-shocks in the running of the universe, in the very plan and purpose of creation.

The Power Of Private Acts

As I said, today it is not necessarily our challenge to die for *kiddush Hashem*. Today, our challenge is to live for *kiddush Hashem* — with our day-to-day lives. And every Jew has a different assignment where and how to make *kiddush Hashem* — the businessman in the business world, the yeshiva-man in the yeshiva world; the career woman in her career, and the housewife in the house; the parents without children and the couple with more children than they can handle; the wealthy person and the poor; the healthy and the sick; the young and the old — no one is ever at any time withheld from making *kiddush Hashem*, because that is the bottom line of our existence in this world.

And that is what makes life — life. That is what makes it more than a series of videos and vacations. That is what makes it meaningful and worth living no matter under what circumstances.

The Rambam, Maimonides, expands our entire concept of *kiddush Hashem* with a profound, far-reaching insight. He writes that a righteous act performed even *when no one else is looking* is a *kiddush Hashem*. In other words, people

AS IN HEAVEN

commonly think that *kiddush Hashem* entails only public sanctification of G–d. That is a misconception. *Kiddush Hashem* is not only when I go outside and do something which makes others say, "Look how great a Jew is." *Kiddush Hashem* can take place even when no one else is looking, when it is only you alone with G–d.

For instance, a husband comes home and makes a nasty remark. His wife can return the favor with a sharp comeback herself. Moreover, the husband really deserves it. Instead, however, the wife remains quiet. Or it can be the wife who says the remark. Or your in-laws. Or your neighbor. And you can really give it back to them. But you stay quiet and calm because you know it would be a *chillul Hashem* to make a big scene or to hurt the person back. That is a private *kiddush Hashem*. Only G–d knows how hard it was for you to hold your tongue and wait for the bad feeling to pass and be forgiven. That's a great *kiddush Hashem*.

In my opinion, it is these types of private *kiddush Hashems* which are revolutionizing our world today. Tens of thousands of *baalei teshuva* — young people from the most alienated circumstances — are springing up all over the place like mushrooms. Many people ask how they all of a sudden get the desire to become religious. In my opinion, they get it from all the *kiddush Hashems* made in private. Your private act reverberates through the heavens and touches an alienated Jew, sitting alone in the privacy of his room, who decides to reconsider his roots.

SO ON EARTH

Picture it this way. You are probably reading this is in a well-lit room. The light is coming from a generator operated by the local utility company. The generator is not seen. It is far away, inside a building, encased in machinery, yet it is producing the power to light not only this room but hundreds of thousands of other rooms. So, too, a private *kiddush Hashem*. It can have as much power as, if not more power than a *kiddush Hashem* in front of a large crowd of people. All of a sudden, an alienated Jew on a college campus in Atlanta or Texas wakes up one morning and decides to try out a weekend at a Torah retreat.

Let me tell you a true story. A few years ago, I was on my way to give a seminar in Atlanta, Georgia. My flight was scheduled to depart at 12:30, but was delayed three hours. The terminal was stuffy and congested with people. I sat down and thought to myself as follows: "*Hashem*, You gave me a mission to teach Torah to people in Atlanta. If my mission is to get to Atlanta, to give a seminar, then this time is wasted, and my mission is a failure. However, my real mission is to make a *kiddush Hashem* no matter where I am. You have merely given me a different mission: to be stuck in a hot, stuffy airport for a few hours. Since You are in my life even now, every moment is a potential goal in itself. Therefore, I will sit here, serve You, say my prayers, and turn this into a productive situation."

What did I really gain by sitting there? Sunday, at the completion of the seminar, an 18-year old boy with a pony tail came over to me and said, "Rabbi, you really impressed me. And because of you I made a decision to go to Israel to learn in a yeshiva for one year." Then he said to me, "You know what impressed me the most? Your story about the three hour delay in the airport. I realized what it means to live a Jewish life — that every minute is meaningful."

People often make a mistake when they think life is only valuable if they can make something out of it. When things look dim or hopeless — in some way their dreams seem to be snuffed out — they give up. They do not realize that every moment of life, no matter under what circumstances it comes, is an opportunity to accomplish some form of *kiddush Hashem*.

I lecture a lot to childless couples, who particularly need to understand this point. G–d commands us to have children. Now, why does He have to make it a commandment: Isn't it greater for people to want to have children voluntarily of their own free will without being commanded? However, every commandment is a divine mission. And this makes not only the end result a goal, but *every step during the process* of fulfilling the commandment a goal itself as well.

For instance, if everything goes well a pregnant woman lives through nine months of morning sickness, discomfort, and mood swings which finally culminate in excruciating labor pains. Despite all the discomfort, in the end she looks at the newborn and says it was all worth it. What if, however, she was pregnant for a few months and then, G–d forbid, miscarried? How devastating! Or what if the child is

SO ON EARTH

born crippled or retarded? Or what if it is a healthy child who grows up into a real problem child? What will the mother think, then? That all the pain and effort was for nothing.

It does not have to be so, however. Our mission is to perform *kiddush Hashem* — to do whatever G–d demands of us at that moment. If you perform the responsibility of that moment, then — mission accomplished! Consider the pregnant woman who miscarried. She can say to herself: "G–d, You commanded me to have children. It is my business to try and fulfill that commandment. However, I have no guarantee about the end result. I know that as long as I am taking all the necessary steps to fulfill this mission, then I am a success — mission accomplished." When she can say "mission accomplished" and mean it, she will never be devastated. In fact, every second she is pregnant it is as if she is giving birth to a child. Her feeling of accomplishment is not dependent on the final outcome, which is really only in G–d's hands anyway.

We do not have to focus on what will be. We only have to worry about what we are doing *this* moment. If I am doing what G–d really wants me to do this moment — "mission accomplished."

A Moment Really Is Priceless

Let me tell you one more story which gets right to the heart of the issue. A few years ago, an 18-year-old young man learning in a yeshiva in England came down with cancer. He became so sick that his doctors told him that chemotherapy wouldn't work. They advised the family to take him home from the hospital in order to live out his last days in peace. The boy was very sick. The family didn't give up, however. They brought him to America and found a medical center not far from my home. In fact, the family ended up staying at my son-in-law's house.

"Under ordinary circumstances nothing can be done," the doctors told them. "However, there is a new type of experimental therapy which — although very painful — probably will extend his life a month or two." The doctors insisted, though, that they would only go ahead with the therapy if the patient signed a paper taking full responsibility for the procedure. The parents, in turn, asked a great Torah authority whether their son was allowed to or even obligated to take on this therapy. He mulled over all the details and told them that, in their particular case, the only one who could make the final decision was the son himself.

Shortly afterward, the father called me up and told me his son wanted to speak with me. I came over and the boy asked his parents to step out for a short while so he could consult with me alone.

"I know I am going to die soon," he told me, "And I have no complaints against G–d, even though I don't understand why this situation has come upon me. I am not afraid. The thing that bothers me most is that my family will be pained. However, if this is what G–d wants I accept it wholeheartedly.

SO ON EARTH

"Nevertheless," he continued, "I have been told about this therapy which may extend my life an extra month or so, and that the decision to take it or not is completely up to me. My question to you is: What am I accomplishing by living an extra month? I am already helpless, lying here connected to all these tubes; I can't concentrate more than five minutes at a time. My family will lose a son, but wouldn't it be inflicting more agony on them by seeing me in this state for an extra month? What should I do?"

First, I told him that I hoped he didn't expect me to make the decision for him. He concurred. Then, I told him the only thing I could do, perhaps, was to educate him how much living an extra month was worth. If he understood how much it was worth, then he could make a more informed decision.

I began the conversation by asking him to tell me which commandment was the greatest in the entire Torah. Eventually, I got him to agree that the commandment of life is the greatest. The Torah tells us *chai behem*, to "live by them (i.e., by the commandments)." Life is the greatest commandment because the commandment to "live by them" tells us we must transgress the Torah if a situation arises where keeping a commandment puts our life in danger. If you are on a deserted island, for instance, and you can only survive by eating pork, not only are you permitted to eat it but you are obligated to do so.

I then went on and related to him a discussion in Torah law which, although hypothetical, sheds light on this issue.

AS IN HEAVEN

"Imagine a very old person in a vegetative state on his death bed in the hospital, and doctors guarantee the family they can extend his life one extra moment, but the procedure requires that every Jew in the world transgress all the commandments (excluding murder, adultery, and idolatry, which are the three exceptions to the commandment to 'live by them'). I know it is completely hypothetical," I told him, "but imagine such a case, and we know that the doctors are telling the truth: instead of dying at 100 years of age, the old person in the vegetative state will die at 100 plus one moment if all Jews do something like eat pork on Yom Kippur. What does Torah law dictate in such a circumstance? The answer is that not only would it be permitted to transgress in that case, but one *must* transgress to add on that extra moment.

"This Torah law," I told him, "is revealing to us how much a moment of life is worth. G–d is telling us that even though He created the world so that we could keep all the commandments in the Torah, nevertheless if even one person in a vegetative state can gain one extra moment of physical life through temporarily suspending the fulfillment of those commandments, then He prefers we suspend them. That is how valuable a moment of this life is to Him.

"Take a deep breath," I said to the young man. "King David wrote: Every soul (*neshama*) thanks G–d. By changing the vowel of the second word the verse can be read: Every breath (*neshima*) thanks G–d. Every breath of air is an extra second of life, and a second of our life gives G–d

SO ON EARTH

unimaginable returns. Think about it. We, with our limited intellects, cannot truly comprehend how G–d gets anything by our living, but He must get something unimaginable if He is willing to have virtually His entire Torah transgressed for one person to gain one extra moment of life. A single breath is the song of the life, even if that life may be experiencing unbearable pain or existing in a vegetative state.

"You ask me," I told him, "what you can accomplish by extending your life an extra month. I ask you: Do you realize how much G–d is willing to sacrifice so that you should live an extra moment? I am not telling you what to do, but deciding to take on the extra therapy is a declaration to the world that life, in any form, is the most precious gift. You would be showing us how a person about to lose life is willing to pay the highest price possible for more life. After all, you would not be doing it for yourself, because you are not afraid to die; and you would not be doing it for your family, because they only suffer more by seeing you in this state. You would be doing it only because G–d told you what a moment of life is worth to Him. It is a declaration to G–d that the opportunity to take a few more breaths of the life He gave you is your ultimate motivation for living.

"Unfortunately," I concluded, "many of us are simply existing. We complain about all the things wrong in our lives. We are insensitive. We don't really know what life is. We don't appreciate the value of a moment. Since, however, you have no other choice but to face reality, and fight

AS IN HEAVEN

for every moment of life, you can teach us about life. And, if you do — you are our teacher."

In the end, he made the decision to take the therapy. A few days later, his father came to me excitedly and asked, "What did you tell him? What did you tell him? He is always smiling. The doctors can't get over how well he takes the therapy. They ask me if I know why. I told them that he's been like this ever since he talked with you. Rabbi, what did you tell him? Did you hypnotize him or something?" I assured the father that I did nothing more than teach him the Torah outlook on life.

Now, this boy was very sick, as I said, but to the doctors' surprise, during that extra month, he became well enough to take leave of the hospital for a while. He ended up staying at my daughter's house. I visited him there, and he explained to me that sometimes when he got severe pains he could not concentrate enough to remember what I had told him. He took out a tape recorder and asked me to repeat everything. He also wanted to include on the tape answers to some new questions which had since come to his mind.

For instance, one question was that, as the Talmud teaches, even the most evil of evil people do not suffer in *Gehinnom* (Purgatory or Hell) more than the equivalent of twelve months. Yet, the boy asked me, he was already into the thirteenth month of his illness. My answer to him was that in *Gehinnom* you are cleansing your soul; here, in this life, you are expanding your soul, you are making your soul more of what it is. This life is a time of producing; in the afterlife you reap, but you do not sow new seeds. That is why the Talmud says that a moment of life here is worth more than the entire existence in the afterlife. When he heard this, a huge smile spread across his face.

After a short while, he had to return to the hospital. He listened to the recording constantly. The doctors and nurses couldn't understand how he was always so happy. They didn't realize it, but his secret was that he truly appreciated life. He wasn't hypnotized. We're hypnotized. He was clear. He was living.

On the Sabbath before Passover he left this world, but even then it was with a smile on his face.

True happiness results from the awareness of converting every moment into a fulfillment of the ultimate purpose. This young man converted breath after breath from this life into eternal life while right here! He was making a *kiddush Hashem*, the greatest kind of *kiddush Hashem*.

Tznius — The Most Crucial Challenge Today

During the Holocaust the challenge was to make a *kiddush Hashem* and say *Yisgadal vayiskadash shmay rabbah* . . . . Nowadays, in my opinion, the greatest challenge facing this generation is in the area of *tznius* ("modesty," or "inwardness," i.e. being true to one's most creative, inner self, as we are about to explain). Both women and men have to be *tznius*, but, generally speaking, with different areas of emphasis.

AS IN HEAVEN

For a man, the *bris*, the circumcision, is the symbol of his responsibility to act with *tznius* — he must be modest in the way he uses his strongest, most creative urge. He must circumcize that urge. A woman, on the other hand, has an equally strong urge, but it manifests itself primarily as the desire to show off her beauty. For a woman, then, dressing modestly, in accordance with Jewish law, is her fundamental way of fulfilling her responsibility to act in a *tznius* way.

Now, it is obvious that the entire concept of *tznius* — especially for women — is under direct and aggressive "enemy assault" in today's general society. King Solomon said, *kol kevuda bas melech p'nima*, "All the glory of the king's daughter is inside." But in today's world, where even the most traditional Jewish women enter the workforce to allow their *kollel* husbands to continue learning, does this idea have practical relevance? These Jewish women are not *p'nim*, "inside" — they are *chutz*, "outside." Therefore, do we have to concede that King Solomon's teaching is not really applicable to today's situation?

NO.

We need not give up one inch of *kol kevuda bas melech p'nima*. We can be just as "inside" as our grandparents were. The first thing we have to do, though, is understand the true meaning of insularity. Years ago the definition of inwardness and insularity was physical isolation — there was a literal wall, a literal town boundary. Today, however, a brick wall does not insulate at all. You can live in the most insular community and yet allow the filth of Times

SO ON EARTH

Square into the privacy of your house — and, moreover, nobody outside will know about it. We cannot consider ourselves insular any longer merely because we live in a certain physical environment. Today the *chutz* penetrates to the deepest, deepest bastions of *p'nim*.

At the same time, the reverse must also be true. If "Times Square" can penetrate into a Jewish home — into a Jewish *mikdash me'at* (a miniature sanctuary) — then a *mikdash me'at* can penetrate into Times Square! How? Can we really maintain our *tznius*, our inwardness and modesty, when we are forced to venture into the outside world? Yes. The answer is by remembering our purpose there: To make *kiddush Hashem*, to "sanctify the Name of G–d."

We Jews cannot help but be high profile. A Jewish businessman usually is the best in his field. A Jewish lawyer usually is best in his field. A Jewish doctor usually is the best in his field. And, unfortunately, a Jewish criminal is also usually the best in his field. But wherever we are, whoever we are, we have one purpose: to make *kiddush Hashem*.

Yes, even a Jewish criminal can perform *kiddush Hashem*.

I have the privilege to speak to a "captive" audience of Jewish prisoners in a high security prison in upstate New York. And I must tell you that some of them have developed beautifully in the past three or four years. They thought they were totally worthless serving time there. "You are not serving time," I tell them. "You are producing

AS IN HEAVEN

time. You are here for the same purpose I am: to make a *kiddush Hashem*, to sanctify the name of G–d. Of course, you made your mistakes. But do not think you were put in here because your judge was an anti-Semite or your lawyer was incompetent. There are many people who did what you did, were brought to trial, and nevertheless got away scot free. You are here," I tell them, "because G–d sent you here. Therefore, you should find G–d here. You should find yourself." And many of them do.

We Jews are a high profile people: in businesses, in hospitals, in bankruptcy courts, and in prisons. We cannot avoid it. G–d wants us out in the world. The point is, though, that in the final analysis He put us there for one reason: to make a *kiddush Hashem* wherever we are. This is the attitude a Jewish professional or businessperson must develop.

Zevulun was the tribe of merchants blessed to work in partnership with the tribe of Yissachar, allowing the latter to remain insular in a learning environment for their entire lives. Today, too, we are divided into Zevuluns and Yissachars.[9] It does not make sense, though, to say that Zevulun was designated to operate in the work-world because G–d had no choice but to use him as a pawn in keeping Yissachar insular. G–d can do anything. In actuality, then, Zevulun must be out in the business world for a positive reason — because Torah has to be disseminated out to the business world and Zevulun is the one designated to do it; he is there to make a *kiddush Hashem*.

SO ON EARTH

A Zevulun must realize that G–d put him there specifically because He wants him to perform a mission in Manhattan — in Wall Street, 47th Street, in Times Square — no less than he wants the Yissachar to perform a mission in the four walls of the yeshiva. Moreover, as long as he stays cognizant that he is in the workplace to perform the commandment of *kiddush Hashem* he is surrounded by a special aura of protection, for the Talmud says, "The agents of a *mitzvah* will not be harmed." An agent, by definition, is someone who nullifies his will to the sender's will — who, in effect, becomes an extension of the sender. A *mitzvah*-commandment is the express will of G–d. The more a Zevulun-type makes himself a whole-hearted agent of G–d's will the more worthy he is to receive special Divine protection.

This is the point: by always remembering that your one, true goal is to perform the commandment of *kiddush Hashem,* in whatever circumstance you find yourself in, then you create and maintain a *tznius*, insular, inward, *p'nim* state-of-mind. Yes, you can take it with you wherever you go. If you are perforce exposed to the excesses of the business-world you should repeat to yourself that you are there for one primary reason: to represent G–d, to be *mekadaish shaim Shamayim,* to "sanctify the name of heaven." If you reach the point where you become an actual extension of G–d, then you will find the strength to overcome the obstacles and remain properly inward.

🍎 AS IN HEAVEN

A Personal Experience

I was raised in a very protected environment. It is a credit to my parents and teachers. And I continued to create a physically insular environment around myself as much as possible. For years, however, I had to commute into 47th Street. I had to park my car on 8th Avenue, in the worst section, and walk through several blocks of filth just to get to work. One day it dawned on me that after a *Shabbos* in Monsey, and a Sunday immersed in learning, you need not feel *chutz* ("outside") — you can still be *p'nim* ("inside"). When the full impact of this thought struck me, instead of commuting into work with a defensive attitude I realized that I and all the busloads of Jews who were arriving from the Five Boroughs and their environs were soldiers zeroing in on "enemy territory."

Davening. Learning. Acting with integrity. Creating *kiddush Hashem*. We were literally an army of commandos penetrating the forty-ninth level of *tumah* — the most exposed, "defiled" sections of New York City. Moreover, for decades we soldiers were making this penetration. We were (and are) making *kiddush Hashem,* and using our money to set up *Yeshivas,* Bais Yaakov schools, charity organizations, etc. Our children learn in advanced institutions all over the world. This is not just a defensive stance. This is where some of the most pitched battles for the soul of the Jewish People are being fought.

I am not saying this is easy. Maintaining the *p'nim* state-of-mind in the outside world may require the willpower,

SO ON EARTH

cunning, and ingenuity of a commando. Still, it is possible to learn very fast how to accomplish great things in our own small ways. It all begins, though, with our minds. We have ultimate control over this battlefield. And the momentum of the overall "war effort" may depend on you and your next encounter with the enemy. If you remember that *tznius* boils down to a state of mind, then you have the ammunition not only to survive the battle, but to make a very real and significant impact on the war effort.

(It is important that what I say is neither misunderstood nor left open for distortion, so let me add that I am not proposing that a seminary student give up her ideals of becoming a teacher so she can have the opportunity to "make a *kiddush Hashem* in Manhattan." I am not saying that a scholar should leave the four walls of his physically insular environment to become a businessman. What I am saying is that for those who already find themselves in the work-world, or who are properly advised to enter a business or profession, for such people your accomplishments — your spiritual accomplishments — can be enormous.)

Bringing It All Together

As you will notice, this opening chapter is by far the longest one in the book — and the most important. We cannot talk about the Bible, the Torah, philosophy, etc. if we do not know the meaning of life and what we are doing here. The Torah tells us that we are here for a purpose. We are here to bring G–d into this world, to make this world a reflection of heaven.

Of course, to really know that G–d exists means to live a life that is consistent with that knowledge. We can't intellectually acknowledge G–d and then act as if He does not exist. Attaining consistency — congruence between what we believe and the way we act — is not easy to create or maintain. Yet it is possible.

We have no chance, though, if we do not even know the "magic word" of Judaism: *kiddush Hashem*. By always remembering that every moment, no matter under what circumstances, is another opportunity to sanctify the name of our G–d, then we can begin to revolutionize our lives — and from there we can revolutionize the world.

Part II

THE CREATOR

CHAPTER 2

Reality And Illusion

- *Explaining the nature of reality, the light and shadow analogy, the idea of the Ten Sayings with which the world was created, the relationship between the Ten Commandments and the Ten Sayings, and the idea of the Sabbath.*

Several years ago when I first became involved with teaching Judaism to assimilated college students, I often heard them fall back on the same argument: "Nothing is absolute." Never having gone to college myself this was news to me.

"Don't you exist?" I would ask.

"Maybe."

"But you must agree that you are standing here in front of me now?"

"Maybe. Maybe not. Nothing is absolute."

❦ AS IN HEAVEN

It was like talking to a brick wall. I did not know how to respond until one day the words came to me and I replied, "But you must admit you believe in one absolute — the absolute that there are no absolutes."

When I first encountered this attitude, though, I had to ask myself: Where does such nonsense come from? There must be a reason why people have an inclination to believe it. Even nonsense must have a motivation. Then I reminded myself of a line by a great Jewish thinker who said there is no claim in the world which does not have at least some basis in fact, some kernel of truth underneath the surface. When I heard college youth proclaiming that the world is not absolute — that our existence is not absolute — I was eventually able to find a root for the idea in our mystical books.

And, the truth of the matter is — the world does not exist, at least not in the way we normally think of it.

What is the world? It is nothing more than a shadow. A shadow does not exist by itself. It is nothing more than the result of an obstruction of light. Take away the light and there is no shadow. We — and our world — are nothing but shadows of G–d.

The Film Projector and the Shadow

And G–d said, "Let there be light," and there was light. (Genesis 1:3)

SO ON EARTH

How do you make a movie? You take a projector of light and then obstruct the light with a filmstrip. When the light penetrates the film an image comes out the other side onto the screen. In order to create a man with a nice dark suit, or a woman with a nice red dress, you needed darkened film.

This is the way G–d created the world.

In the mystical books G–d is called *Or Ain Sof*, an Endless Light. We do not know what G–d is, of course. Nevertheless, we can call Him "light" because one of the properties of light is to project itself. Film projectors have powerful bulbs which can project light thousands of feet. G–d is an *endless* light. His light illuminates to the lowest depths and farthest distances. There is no spot where the light of G–d does not hit. Take anything that exists — a cup of coffee, for instance. It is a manifestation of the *Or Ain Sof*, of G–d's Endless Light. It is not the raw light, but a concealment of the light expressed as a shadow in the form of a cup of coffee.

G–d is such a master "Film-maker," of course, that His creations are three-dimensional concrete images. And not only that, He imbues His images with free choice. This is what it means to be made in the image of G–d (*tzelem Elokim*). We are endowed with free choice just like G–d has free choice. In fact, He gives us so much free choice that we can even come to believe that we are not shadows, but that we exist independent of G–d!

Man is the one creation made in the Divine Image — and we will discuss this more in detail ahead (Chapter 5). At the same time, however, we are the most heavily obstructed shadow in this filmstrip called the universe.[10] We can say, "There is no such thing as G–d. I am not a shadow. I exist independent of G–d." This is akin to an image on the movie screen all of a sudden saying, "I am not an image on the screen. I do not follow a script. The scenes of my life were not produced beforehand, nor am I under anyone's direction other than my own. No film producer made me."

This is the human condition. We are three-dimensional, concrete shadows who can think we possess independent existence.

Imagine a person born and raised his entire life in a movie theater. From the beginning he grows up facing only the screen, eyes glued to the images there twenty-four hours a day. Never once does he even leave his seat or venture outside. What will he come to think? That all those images on the wall — those people, cars, horses, buildings, trees, mountains, rivers, etc. — are real. If you approach him and say, "You know, the whole world that you think is the world is not really the world. It does not exist. It is a shadow" — if you say that, he will stare at you with glazed eyes or call you a lunatic.

We do not realize it, but we have been born into a movie theater. G–d is the "Endless Light" who projected Himself endlessly to the lowest spot — this physical world. The fact that the earth exists is because G–d is projecting His light right now.

SO ON EARTH

There are no absolutes — at least in regard to "reality" as we usually think of it. The existent world is truly nothing more than a shadow.

The Transformer

The Sages tell us that the world was created with Ten Sayings (*Maamaros*).[11] ("And G–d said, Let there be light" is one saying, for instance.) This means that every object in the world is the result of one of these sayings.

To explain this idea properly, imagine your local electric company and its gigantic generators. An electrical generator produces billions and billions of kilowatts of electricity. In order to make that great energy available for household use, though, it must be reduced by a transformer. A transformer diminishes the voltage so that you can plug your appliance into a wall socket. One transformer, however, is not enough to give your vacuum cleaner the proper amount of electricity. A second transformer, a third transformer, and so on are needed until the energy flowing through the line is safe for household use.

There were Ten Sayings through which the world was created. Each utterance was like a transformer. The original utterance — *beraishis* (the Talmud[12] considers the first word, *beraishis,* a separate utterance) — was infused with such high degrees of "G-dliness" that it needed to be transformed downward into levels usable for His creations. There were ten such "transformers," which are represented

Reality And Illusion 67

AS IN HEAVEN

by the words, "And G–d said . . ." Each one further reduced and transformed the original utterance.

Ten Commandments, Ten Sayings

The world was created with ten sayings. Yet, in contradistinction to this we are taught that "G–d looked into the Torah and created the world."[13] This is a contradiction. Which does the world emanate from: the Ten Sayings or the Torah? The answer is the latter (because the Ten Sayings were said at the time of creation, not beforehand). We can therefore say that the Ten Sayings originate from a "primordial Torah."

The idea of a primordial Torah is something difficult if not impossible for the human mind to grasp. (If it is something which by definition existed before creation, then how can we even have the mental forms or apparatus necessary to conceive of it?) There is, however, something in Jewish experience which serves as a visual form for the primordial Torah: the Ten Commandments, the divine word etched into stone miraculously. The Ten Sayings in reality originate from the Ten Commandments.[14] The Ten Commandments are the true root, the true source, of creation.

Therefore, if the Ten "Sayings" represent *speech*, then the Ten Commandments represent pure *thought*. Speech is by definition a limitation of thought. Even the most articulate human being cannot express his full thought through words. So, too, when G–d came to "express" Himself in the form of creation He perforce expressed a reduced or constricted form of His true being. The Ten Sayings are that form. The Ten Commandments, by contrast, more represent His essence. They are His thought, so to speak.

This helps us understand an otherwise obscure statement by one of the Hasidic masters[15] to the effect that "the Ten Plagues torn asunder the Ten Sayings and revealed the Ten Commandments." The explanation is as follows: Egyptian culture was immersed to an unparalleled degree in moral degradation and abandonment to physical desires. It was the material world, the Ten Sayings, incarnate. Each of the Ten Plagues peeled back one layer of Egypt's overindulgent materialistic lifestyle. When the process was complete the Jewish People were ready to leave Egypt to receive the Ten Commandments on Mount Sinai. Thus, *the Ten Plagues tore asunder the Ten Sayings* (the physical world as represented by Egyptian culture) *which enabled G–d to reveal to the world the Ten Commandments.*

(This is also why Abraham was tested *ten* times. Each test corresponded to one layer of "camouflage" which enabled him to peer at the soul of creation laying underneath.)

We see, then, that sometimes in order to experience the ultimate reality (the Ten Commandments) there must be an intermediate process of something akin to the Ten Plagues or the Ten Tests. This intermediate process entails peeling back or destroying the filmy layer camouflaging the ultimate reality.

AS IN HEAVEN

The Moshol and the Nimshol

Rabbi Yaakov Kaminetzky, *zt'l*, once addressed the question how, as the Sages teach,[16] Abraham knew the Torah even before it was given on Sinai. He explained that the Torah is the blueprint of the world, and just as an architectural expert can perceive the underlying blueprint by looking at an already existing building, so, too, Abraham discovered the Torah before it was given: He perceived the blueprint through observation of "the building," i.e. the world itself.

This is our goal, too. We are here to peel back the Ten Sayings in order to see the Ten Commandments. In simplified terms, this means that we should not become deceived by superficial appearances — by "nature" (i.e. the Ten Sayings) — but peer beneath the surface to see the root (the Ten Commandments). In this sense, our goal is to look beneath the Ten Sayings to find the Ten Commandments.

Another way of explaining this idea is by comparing the difference between the Ten Sayings and the Ten Commandments to the difference between a parable and its moral (the *moshol* and the *nimshol,* respectively). Parables or stories are easy to relate to. Even children (including the child within each of us) enjoys a good story. Yet every parable has its moral.

The Ten Sayings are the parable (*moshol*) and the Ten Commandments are the moral (*nimshol*). The Ten Commandments represent the endless, limitless wisdom of G–d.

SO ON EARTH

The Ten Sayings — physical creation itself — serve as a parable for that Divinity.

We have to understand that the world is nothing more than a parable with a moral, a message. Despite all our daily challenges we have to make it our business to discover the full message behind the veil of the parable. This is what it means to "see the Ten Commandments in the Ten Sayings." The Ten Sayings *camouflage* the Ten Commandments. We must attempt to see behind the camouflage, the curtain, the veil; we must look beyond the storyline and come upon the deeper message. The Ten Commandments are the soul of the Ten Sayings. And life is an exercise to find soul, not just experience body; it is an exercise to grasp the moral, not just enjoy the parable.

The Sabbath

This helps explain the idea of the Sabbath.

> Thus were finished the heaven and the earth and all their host. And G–d completed, on the seventh day, all the work that He had done; and He rested on the seventh day from all the work He had done. (Genesis 2:1-3)

Does G–d need to rest? What, then, was the work G–d "rested" from? The answer is that He rested from camouflaging and concretizing His endless depth into the form of a parable.

By the end of the sixth day, G–d had finished saying the tenth of the Ten Sayings. He stopped reducing and

Reality And Illusion 71

AS IN HEAVEN

constricting His raw essence. The seventh day, Sabbath (which means "to rest"), is the moral of the parable, the soul of the story. It was designed to allow us to get back in touch with the root message of our existence.

How so? As we immerse ourselves in our work six days a week we can easily fall into the trap of thinking that we were the cause of our monetary or materialistic success. On the seventh day, however, we refrain from work and thereby express our belief that all our mundane acts and concerns are ultimately in the hands of our Maker. This is why if we properly keep the Sabbath we naturally feel a profound and deep tranquillity, a *Shabbos menucha*. On the Sabbath we peel back the illusion, the veil of self-accomplishment, to reveal the true underlying root of all our success, indeed the root of all causes, of existence itself: the Creator. And it is this awareness, that our Creator is in control, which produces the peace and tranquillity of the Sabbath.

Thus, for six days we immerse ourselves in our mundane work, which is equivalent to immersing ourselves in the Ten Sayings, the physical creation, the parable. On the seventh day, the Sabbath, we remove ourselves from the parable to reconnect with the moral (the *nimshol*), the message. In essence, for sixth days we live a parable, trying our best to discover the root meaning of our physical, mundane, weekday experiences; we are trying to convert our allotment of earth — i.e. our mundane experiences — into a mirror of heaven.

However, it is not easy. We fall prey to "parable-like" thinking despite our efforts. On the seventh day, though, we get back into direct contact with the root by dropping out, so to speak, of the parable. We untie ourselves from the illusion of the six weekdays.

CHAPTER 3

Coincidence?

- *Explaining the mystery of Divine Providence, its connection to the opening verse of the Torah, the first of the 13 Principles of Faith, the reason life is perceived as meaningful or meaningless, the original light and why it was hidden, the way to access the original light, and a perspective to help understand Jewish suffering.*

I was once invited to deliver a lecture entitled "Mysticism In Everyday Life":

"Probably," I began, "many of you here are asking yourself: Is there such a thing as mysticism to begin with? And if there is, what is it and what does it have to do with me, with my everyday life? All of you, I would venture to guess, have come here to hear something about mysticism. I, on the other hand — when thinking about this topic — think of it from a completely different angle ... Is there such a thing as everyday life?"

SO ON EARTH

Is There Everyday Life?

"With Wisdom G–d created the heaven and the earth." (Targum Yerushalmi to Genesis 1:1)

The Targum Yerushalmi, one of the classic Aramaic translations of the Torah, renders the opening words of the Torah — *Beraishis bara Elokim*, "In the beginning G–d created. . ." — as "With Wisdom G–d created. . ." In simple terms this means that G–d's wisdom is implanted in the world. If you want to comprehend the wisdom of G–d, to whatever small degree it is possible, you do not have to go to the mountains of India or some far off island and meditate all day. If you simply reflect upon your so-called mundane life you will be stunned and fascinated by the great wisdom behind everything happening in it.

And, indeed, if we are honest with ourselves and look backwards to try to put together the links which brought us to where we are today we will perforce be stunned by the innumerable "chance" meetings, wrong turns which turned out to be right turns, and other incidents we thought were coincidence.

We are taught: *eenosh b'eenosh poga*, (literally) "People with people meet [i.e. when two people meet, it is not a coincidence]." Why on any given day of the week will you find people flying from New York to Los Angeles to make money, while at the same time there are people flying from Los Angeles to New York to make money? New York has enough money for the New York businessperson; and Los

❡ AS IN HEAVEN

Angeles has enough money for the Los Angeles businessperson. Why, then, all this traveling back and forth?

On a superficial level you would say, "To make money." In reality, however, the reason is *eenosh b'eenosh poga*: G–d's plan is that people have to meet and interact with each other. Money is the *means*, in G–d's eyes, not the ends. The New York businessperson needs to fly to Los Angeles, and the businessperson in Los Angeles needs to fly to New York, not to make money (even though that is hopefully an outcome), but in actuality because all their moving around, and flying back and forth, is part of the Divine plan to bring different people into contact with each other. G–d just baits them with the money.

Eenosh b'eenosh poga, when two people meet it is not a coincidence. When you meet someone or someone meets you there is a Divine purpose behind the meeting. Nothing is coincidence. Not even the fact that you are reading this book right now at this time. We, therefore, each have a responsibility to ask: Why did G–d bring me in contact with this person, with this book, with this circumstance? And this is the intent behind the statement of our Sages,[17] "Every individual is obligated to say: for my sake the entire world was created." Your first responsibility is to know that the world was created for you, and that everything happens because G–d makes you the center of His attention.

SO ON EARTH

The Mystery of Divine Providence

This is called Divine Providence, or *hashgacha*. And *hasgacha* goes so far, our Sages tell us, that even if you steal just a small coin from another person (and certainly if you steal more) "you are stealing his soul." What do they mean by equating stealing money with "stealing a soul"? The mystical books explain that nothing in this world is coincidence. That small coin was given to that person for a purpose. It is part of a Great Plan. If you steal it, you not only take five cents from him: *you take something that is part of his soul* because it was given to him to fulfill some purpose.

As a survivor of the Holocaust I can tell you that no one survived without a miraculous string of "coincidences." Just to give you a little glimpse about what I am talking about let me tell you one personal story. When the Nazis came to our city and the Jews had to relinquish all their possessions my father took my mother's wedding ring and buried it inside a hollow wall. One day we got word that a boy became sick with tuberculosis and needed to be hospitalized. The family needed money to save his life, so my father and mother dug out the ring and sold it to save the boy. Others said my parents were crazy, but it was a case of *pikuach nefesh*, a Jewish life was endangered.

As it turned out, the boy was admitted to the hospital but shortly thereafter died unfortunately. When he was originally admitted into the hospital, however, he was not allowed to do so under his own name. Instead he needed an alias, so he used my father's name. When the boy died the death certificate was issued in my father's name. Not long after this my father received orders to report to a work camp. My mother simply sent in a copy of the death certificate and my father's life was saved.

This is called mysticism in everyday life. And there are many, many "everyday" situations and circumstances happening to us all the time — which we cannot say we planned — which make monumental impacts on our lives. Moreover, these coincidences have been happening since we were little children. The problem is that we do not give ourselves time to reflect and think about their meaning in order to thereby gain the deep conviction that our lives are part of a great Divine Script. We are so busy pushing and pushing to "get ahead" that we rarely, if ever, take the time think about anything. We set goals, pursue them — even attain them — and then find ourselves disappointed and empty. So we set new goals, pursue them, attain them — and still feel we are missing something. So we set new goals. And so on. Our entire life becomes one chain of goal-setting and disappointments, goal-setting and disappointments, because we never take the time to stop and think.

I frequently repeat the findings of a study made years back which reported that only one percent of people actually think; four percent of people think they think; and ninety-five percent of people would rather die than think. You do not need a degree to think. (A degree only perhaps

SO ON EARTH

earns you entry into the second category: people who think they think. But that is all.) Your first priority is to become a real thinker.

"With Wisdom G–d created the heaven and the earth." Even if we cannot all be Talmudic scholars and mystics, we can perceive some inkling at least of the Divine Plan if we just take the time to think about what has happened to us in the past and what is happening to us right now.

Confessions of an Economist

Years ago, a brilliant secular Jew, a Professor of Economics, was sent by the American government as an advisor to a country in Central America. Some natives in the mountains there asked him his religion.

"I'm Jewish," he replied.

"Are you religious? Do you pray to G–d?" they asked.

"No."

"How come? Don't you realize how beautiful your religion is?"

To make it short, that "coincidental" encounter woke him up and spurred him to find out more about Judaism. Eventually, he came to my town and was a guest by me for his first Sabbath experience.

"What do you do?" I asked.

"I'm an Economist," he replied.

"I don't understand," I said. "What does an Economist do? I mean, I consider myself an Economist — in the practical sense. You see, I have a large family and have to figure out how to feed them. What does it mean to be a professional Economist, though?"

"Well, you see," he responded, "I work for the American government. Most of the time I sit down with other Economists and plan the country's future."

"What do you plan?"

"Things like the flow of money, the prime rate, the interest rate, inflation, recession, taxes, tax-cuts, etc. — everything that will improve the economy of the government."

"Tell me honestly," I said looking him squarely in the eyes, "did it ever happen that even one of your plans worked out just as it was planned?" He laughed. "Why are you laughing?" I asked.

"To tell you the truth, it never once worked out the way we planned. In fact, it always goes the opposite way. We plan right; it goes left. We plan left; it goes right. It never works out. If you want to know the truth," he added, "we make bets between ourselves who will be the least farthest from reality."

Eventually I got him to admit to a statement made long, long ago by King Solomon: "The heart of the king and his ministers is in the hand of G–d." If the best concocted plans of "the king and his ministers" are nevertheless still in the hands of G–d, then certainly the plans of commoners like the rest of us are in G–d's hands. He maneuvers everything to come out the way He wants it.

SO ON EARTH

He Did, Does, And Will Do

And G–d said, "Let there be light." And there was light. (Genesis 1:3)

G–d is called the "Endless Light" (see Chapter 2). What makes light an acceptable metaphor for G–d? Light must be continuous; it must be generated this moment. The light you see now is no longer the light of a moment ago. The instant the source is turned off the light is discontinued. A table, by contrast, is not like that. The moment the carpenter completes it and walks away it continues as a table.

Creation is not like a table; it is *not* here now because G–d created it long ago. If G–d should cease His "flow of electricity" into us for even one instant we will cease to exist. We are not here because G–d gave us intrinsic existence many years ago. We are here now — this moment, as you read these very words — because He wants us to exist even now. The events of every moment are completely in His hands.

This is why nothing is coincidence. In the deepest sense, the physical world is really only the outer garb for an inner, spiritual essence. And that spiritual essence is nothing but the Creator's will. We can recognize and live up to it, or we can try to deny and defy it, but we cannot escape it. G–d runs the world.

Indeed, this is the first principle of Judaism:

> "I believe with perfect faith that the Creator, blessed be His name, is the Creator and Driving Force of all the

creatures. He alone did, does, and will do all things that come to pass."

The above is the first of Maimonides famous Thirteen Principles Of The Jewish Faith. "He alone did, does, and will do all things that come to pass." The world — and every thing, as well as every happening, in it — exists now because G–d desires it to exist now. This is why nothing happens by coincidence. G–d recreates each moment. He pumps into each moment renewed Desire, brand new Will.

This presents us with a great challenge. In fact, it is one of the most difficult challenges we as human beings confront. On one hand, we must be assertive, use our talents, take initiative, and be responsible for our lives. On the other hand, *at the same time,* we must acknowledge that everything is orchestrated by G–d, planned out, planted in our hearts, and placed in our paths as part of a Great Plan.

This is a paradox, admittedly. We have free will, yet simultaneously everything is foreseen and planned beforehand.[18] None of our best efforts — to do good or bad — would come to fruition if not for G–d. Even the thoughts of our hearts are in His hands. "But," you say, "I want to do this. I want to do that. I am in complete control." True, we are all driven to do certain things, but where did our drives originate from? Did we give birth to ourselves, and choose our tastes and preferences? Obviously not. And what, ultimately, are our drives dependent upon? "He is the Driving Force . . . He alone did, does, and will do all things that come to pass."

SO ON EARTH

You have free will, yet your free will does not negate the fact that He is in control. This is the paradox. Our rational minds tell us it can only be one way or the other. G–d, however, is not limited to our rational minds. He gave us free will, and at the same time "He alone did, does, and will do all things that come to pass."[19]

When we truly believe this first principle — and not just intellectually acknowledge it — then "everyday life" takes on an entirely new meaning. If G–d's will, the essence of reality, is behind everything, then there must be a value to everyday life; there must be a meaning in every moment of our lives. Every footstep we take is planned and supervised by a Superior Wisdom — a Wisdom, as the Targum Yerushalmi taught, which permeates Creation. Every person, every place, and every time in "reality" has an inner meaning.

On the other hand, if we have not yet come to understand or believe — or even truly inculcate within ourselves — the First Principle Of Faith, then we will experience much (if not all) of life as meaningless. We will have no choice but to seek to escape into a movie theater, a romance novel, a fantasy vacation; or become unnaturally self-absorbed in a career, a project, a superficial lifestyle — because deep down we believe that everyday life in itself is meaningless and we are not accomplishing anything with it.

The minute we truly believe, on the other hand, that there is a Creator, then nothing in this world can be ignored — no happy event, and no sad event. Nothing can be ignored because it is not haphazard. It is all part of a meaningful design.

The Hidden Light

> And G-d said, "Let there be light." And there was light. (Genesis 1:3)

The Sages inform us that the original light was *not* like the light we experience today. It shined throughout the first seven days of creation (day and night), but was then "hidden away."[20] In fact, when the original light was withdrawn at the end of the first Sabbath, and the darkness of night descended upon the world for the first time, Adam panicked, thinking the world was going to come to an end. He managed to light a fire — which we commemorate every Sabbath conclusion in *havdalah* — and then awoke the next morning, Sunday, for the first time to the light of the sun: i.e. the light independent of the original light. However, the light we call "light" today — the sun's light — *is only an imitation of the real thing; it is not the same as the light of "Let there be light."* That light, the original light, was hidden away and will be restored for the righteous to benefit from in the World To Come.[21]

On a deeper level the symbolic meaning of hiding the original light was the creation of free will. Light is a symbol for G-d's will and therefore when He hid the light it means He put a restriction on His will, so that humankind would not be engulfed in it to the point that they would have no option other than to perform G–d's will. By creating darkness — and, more to the point: by creating spiritual darkness, i.e. denial of G–d, evil — He created the possibility to choose between light and darkness, between good and evil, between G–d's will and "not G–d's will."[22]

This explains the deeper intent of the statement that G–d "hid it [the original light] away for the righteous in the future to come." In place of this original light He gave us the light as we know it. This light is not as powerful. It can be engulfed by darkness. Spiritually, it can appear as if G–d's Presence is completely hidden. And, indeed, we see that evil can seemingly conquer. A Hitler can arise, conquer half the world, and perpetrate a Holocaust. This possibility came into being when G–d "hid away" the original light and replaced it with the light we have today. It made it possible for darkness to not only exist but to seemingly reign, if unopposed.

The question arises — and this is particularly perplexing to some people nowadays — if everything is the result of G–d's will how can evil exist? Can evil in any way be ascribed to His will? In response, bad events are not evil given the long view of life and history. They are, in fact, necessary stages toward revelation of the ultimate good.

Consider a suspense movie. The object of all but the last five minutes of the movie is to keep people on the edge of their seats, to make them cry, to make them scared. They know, they believe, they hope things will work out in the end — that is what they paid their money for — but until the final scene they cannot fathom the full design of the plot (if it is a good movie).

So, too, with G–d's design for the "plot" of creation.

We believe and even know that it is all leading toward the highest possible good. Of course, that does not necessarily make our experience of the present difficulties less real. When "bad things" happen to us we are not expected to deny the pain. Still it is no contradiction to say we have faith that it is all an intricately woven part of the Divine Script. We trust the Author knows what He is doing.

We have to understand, then, that darkness and evil are only made possible because of G–d's will (either because He wills it, or because He decided to give the forces of darkness temporary free reign). He knowingly wove their existence into the fabric of creation.[23]

This allows us to comprehend the true dynamic behind Jewish suffering. The Jewish People are here to be a "light unto the nations,"[24] *to unsheathe the original light* and spread it to the four corners of the earth. We have been sent into the world to banish the darkness. And therefore we have a mission to perform in precisely those areas where darkness reigns supreme.

For a Jew to complete his mission he has to possess the faith that no matter how dark "reality" seems he has been given special insight and tools to divine the truth that everything which transpires is a manifestation of the Divine Will. The source of a Jew's faith is the original light hidden in his soul. It gives him the ability to see G–d in his day-to-

SO ON EARTH

day ordeals, to see that there is no reality except G–d. It gives him a special ability to discover G–d, which is the name of the game, even amidst times of darkness and concealment.

The Labor Pains of Faith

G–d runs the world. If you made a mistake it is really He who led you to making that mistake because He saw that the "mistake" would somehow be better for your ultimate good. If someone insults or injures you it is G–d who allowed him and you to be in the same situation for that insult or injury to happen. Again, G–d does so only for the ultimate good.

This — the idea that G–d's will is behind everything — is the real meaning of faith.

Having faith does not mean one is numb to pain. It is like giving birth to a child. The woman about to give birth is experiencing very real labor pains, yet she knows that after the baby is born she will feel that it was all worth it. That faith in the ultimate outcome gives her the strength to withstand the present pain.

The truth is that every person who goes through pain is delivering a "baby" — that "baby" is yourself. It is the accomplishment that you have remained true to the higher reality — that G–d is behind everything, all for your ultimate good — in the face of extreme hardship. In other words, you have chosen light over darkness.

❦ AS IN HEAVEN

This is the deeper lesson behind the words, "Let there be light." Let there be light in our minds even when all else seems dark. If you learn to see G–d in this world of diminished light, then you will be worthy to see Him in the world entirely bathed in His unique, original light — a light that was hidden just for you.

CHAPTER 4

Staying Connected

- *Explaining the symbolism of water, the idea of mikvah, a definition of holiness, water as a symbol for Torah, the importance of set times for Torah study, the definition of a ben-Torah, and the Ark today.*

And G–d said, "Let there be a sky in the midst of the waters, and let it divide between water and water." And G–d made the sky, and separated the water from under the sky from the waters which were above the sky. And so it was. And G–d called the sky, *shamayim* (heaven). And there was evening and there was morning, a second day. (Genesis 1:6-8)

The second day of creation saw a division between the upper waters and the lower waters. Note that the events of this day are the only ones which are not stamped with the words: "And G–d saw that it was good." The reason is explained by the Sages: Any time a separation takes place, this cannot be called good.[25] (The separation here was that the "upper waters" became associated with *heaven* while the "lower waters" became associated with *earth*.) Indeed,

AS IN HEAVEN

it seemed unfair. As in all arguments one side felt cheated. The "lower waters," so to speak, had a legitimate complaint: "Why were we excluded from heaven?"

The cure, however, was prepared before the illness. Prior to the division, G–d had done something which gave meaning to the seemingly unjust division.

> ... and the spirit of G–d hovered above the face of the waters. (Genesis 1:2)

By stating (on the first day) that the spirit of G–d "hovered" over the waters — i.e. even over the "lower waters," the waters which are part of the earth — the Torah is telling us that G–d's spirit never completely left the physical, material earth. No matter how far the earthly would be from the heavenly an element of the heavenly would always remain in it. Consequently, as long as the "lower waters" would remain original — i.e. undetached from their natural sources (and thereby fit for a *mikvah*; see below) — they would always retain an intrinsic connection to the "upper waters." Indeed, they would be a source of heaven down on earth and have the power to make the impure pure.[26]

Mikvah

This leads to the idea of *mikvah*. A *mikvah* is a body of unpolluted water still connected to its origins. Oceans, rivers, streams, rain water in its natural basin — these are the "lower waters" which constitute an authentic *mikvah*.

SO ON EARTH

The core idea of immersing in a *mikvah* is as follows: Since a human being cannot live under water, then by immersing in that water he is temporarily severing his connection to earthly life.²⁷ This enables him to reestablish the proper reorientation toward the physical, for during the course of our lives it is easy to become *overly* immersed in the physical to our detriment. *Mikvah* is designed to remedy that.

Natural waters — waters which still retain that quality of G–d's spirit hovering over them — reorient and reconnect a person toward heaven even while here on earth. Immersion in the *mikvah* expresses a person's willingness to reconnect with the source of heavenly life through temporarily but completely surrendering his connection to earthiness. Doing so disentangles him from whatever negative effect the physical had had, and enables him to reconnect with the heavenly before going about the task of his work on earth. The larger message of the *mikvah*, therefore, is that even the most unholy, alienated person can always choose to reconnect himself to heavenly values, to holiness.

A Definition of Holiness

This brings up a question: How do we define holiness? One answer is: connecting to the greater portion and/or deeper aspect of your own soul.

Each person has a soul. That does not mean, however, that the entire soul is in you, so to speak. Mystically, a simple person may only be connected to or aware of the "heel" of his soul. The majority of the soul is still connected *only* to heaven. A truly holy person, on the other hand, is connected to a much greater proportion of his soul.

The more a person works on becoming holy the more the remainder of his soul comes into him. Similarly, the Talmud tells us that on the Sabbath we get an "additional soul." It does not necessarily mean a second soul or an attachment to the soul. It means rather that the person gets connected to a higher portion of his *own* soul. This is literally what it means to be in touch with one's soul.

Earthly life, though, is enemy territory for the soul. It cuts us off from our own higher self. The problem is that we must partake of the earthly in order to do what we are here for; we must engage the "enemy" on his own territory. To do so successfully, we need to continually deepen and broaden our connection to our own soul before immersing in the potentially constricting task of sanctifying the earthly.

Consider the act of immersing in a *mikvah* before one's wedding night. Marriage is consummated in the most physically, intimate manner. According to Torah law, the woman must first immerse herself in the *mikvah* before the wedding night. In so doing she is preparing herself to transform the most earthly of earthly acts into a vehicle which will create the highest connection to heaven. The *mikvah*, therefore, helps the couple recognize that even the most physical of earthly acts can become an act of holiness if one

SO ON EARTH

is first properly oriented — i.e. connected to the heavenly — beforehand.

Immersion in the *mikvah* is equivalent to dipping in heaven. The body that comes out of the *mikvah* is no longer a spiritually contaminated[28] physical body; it is a vehicle reinfused with heaven. And it is the body, the earthly body, that — as a vessel for the soul — must be pure in order for a person to make spiritual accomplishments in this life.

This perspective, by the way, also helps explain why water was the vehicle used to destroy the world in the time of Noah. The earth had become so corrupt, so disconnected from heaven, that it had to be destroyed. In actuality, it was not so much destroyed through the flood as prepared to be rebuilt. It was as if G–d took the world and dipped it into a great *mikvah*, so to speak. The earth totally surrendered to heaven.

The important thing to remember is that "when you go into the *mikvah* the *mikvah* must go into you." In other words, in order to bring G–dliness into you, you first have to go into the *mikvah* — you have to surrender, you have to physically cease to exist, so to speak. And when you empty yourself of "yourself" you become receptive to G–dliness.

The real goal of *mikvah*, then, is not so much going into it, but what it enables us to let in: heaven, G–dliness. The *mikvah* is only a vehicle, a process, whereby we increase our G–dliness and holiness — whereby we bring heaven into our earthly lives.

Torah: The Real Mikvah

On a deeper level, what the *mikvah* is to the body the Torah is to the mind. (Indeed, Torah is compared to water.[29]) Surrendering our minds to the Torah is the spiritual counterpart of surrendering our bodies to the waters of the *mikvah*. Torah is G–d's teaching, a product of His mind. By immersing ourselves in it we are dipping our minds inside G–d's mind, so to speak. The fiery holiness of His Torah melts all barriers and blockages of the heart.

Like the "lower waters," however, Torah must be connected to its original, unpolluted sources for it to purify. That means it will purify only when seen as an extension of the mind of G–d, the mind into which the one who studies it is willing to immerse and surrender *totally*. It cannot be merely an intellectual endeavor or academic course of study. We refer to Torah learning as an *osek*, literally an "involvement" with one's whole body and soul. The Chazon Ish points out that *osek* can also mean "business." Torah learning must be all-consuming like a person's business.

The challenge for most people is that not everyone can learn Torah full-time for his entire life. At the minimum, therefore, every Jew must strive to be a *ben-Torah*, literally a "son of the Torah," no matter how much or how little time he has to open a book and learn. The definition of a *ben-Torah* does not so much depend on quantity as quality, Rabbi Yitzchak Hutner, *zt'l*, explains.[30] In essence the definition of a *ben-Torah* boils down to one's priority or

SO ON EARTH

orientation, not necessarily the quantity of one's knowledge. If a young man is learning Torah full-time, but really only gets excited when the day is over so that he can make some extra money or read the newspaper, etc. he is not necessarily the ideal *ben-Torah*. On the other hand, it is possible to conceive of a very busy businessman who nevertheless cannot wait for the first free moment so that he can learn Torah — he is a real *ben-Torah*. It is the Torah which excites him, not the business or the politics.

The definition of a *ben-Torah* is not so much determined by what a person feels when the Torah is open in front of him, but by what he feels *after* it is time to close the book. If more than anything he yearns to return to his learning, if his learning replenishes him and from there spreads out to all his earthly endeavors, then he is truly a *ben-Torah*.

It is literally, therefore, a matter of life and death for every Jew to maintain at least a minimal connection to Torah *every day* no matter how involved in other affairs he may be. This is why there is such an emphasis to set "established times of Torah study." It does not matter if it is one hour, one half-hour, ten minutes — even just five minutes — of daily learning. Whatever level you may be on, and as short as it may be, every person who wishes to be a *ben-Torah* must strive to honestly do all that is humanly possible to maintain some connection to Torah.

This is what it means to merge the lower waters with the upper waters, to repair the division caused on the second day of creation. By creating an island of Torah in your daily schedule you maintain your connection to heaven even while existing on the earth. On the other hand, a person who is not seriously involved in learning Torah with established times is in danger of becoming detached from the "original waters." And that is what causes him to feel Jewishly apathetic, cut-off, or fragmented.

The Holy Ark

The Talmud states that "G–d has no dwelling place in His world since the destruction of the Temple except the four *amos*[31] of *halachah* (Jewish law)."[32] Every person is surrounded by a natural four *amos* of space. It is our personal domain no matter where we go. When a person surrenders himself to the *halachah* he is saying that he surrenders himself to G–d. Wherever he goes, wherever he is, he has made G–d his prime informant.

Before Adam's sin the entire world was brimming with G–d's Presence. After he sinned the Divine Presence receded and receded until, practically speaking, it was almost entirely inaccessible. Then the Temple was built, and the Divine Presence returned and came to rest on the four *amos* of the Holy Ark[33] residing in the Holy of Holies. The Tablets of the Ten Commandments (inside the Holy Ark) were our umbilical cord to heaven. With the destruction of the Temple, however, the Ark was hidden away. All that remains today, therefore, is the "four *amos*" of *halachah*, the counterpart to the "four *amos*" of space taken up by the Holy Ark. Everyone who gives up his private domain for

SO ON EARTH

halachah, consequently, is connecting himself to heaven while here on earth. Wherever such a person walks he, so to speak, is bringing the Holy Ark along with him.

As the Waters Cover the Sea

> ... for the earth shall be full of the knowledge of G–d, as the waters cover the sea. (Isaiah 11:9)

When the Messiah comes and the world will attain true peace, then *the entire world* — not just the four *amos* of some individuals — will be filled with G–d's Presence. Until that time it is the responsibility of each individual to transform his personal domain into a place of holiness, and this is accomplished through surrender to G–d's authority.

A Torah person consults the *halachah* first in every situation. In so doing he recreates the space of the Holy Ark all around him. Moreover, he reverses the effects of the first man's sin. Whereas Adam's sin restricted the Divine Presence to one place the one who keeps *halachah* has taken the Divine Presence and spread it out wherever he goes. In that sense he is repairing the damage of the first man's sin and preparing the world for the coming of the Messiah — when the spirit of G–d will encompass the world "as the waters cover the sea."

Part III

PARTNER WITH THE DIVINE

CHAPTER 5

The Divine Image

- *Explaining the creation of man, a human being as a tree, the higher destiny of being human, what it means to serve G–d, the meaning of Israel, partners with G–d, and how Abraham came to embody the potential Adam never fulfilled.*

Everything in the Torah is meant to teach us something important. On the third day of creation the Torah tells us that G–d made the trees and vegetation. What great relevance does this information contain? The key to the answer is supplied later when the Torah calls the human being "a tree of the field."[34]

One of the deeper implications of telling us about the creation of trees is to teach us about the make-up of the human being. A human being is a tree. A tree is a trunk of wood with roots in the ground which draw up minerals in order to transform them into fruit. So, too, a human being. We are a piece of heaven — a soul — rooted like a tree trunk — a body — in the earth whose mission is to draw

AS IN HEAVEN

forth from the earth spiritual "minerals" in order to produce fruits up high on the branches. This means that we are here to convert even the most physical aspects of our material existence into spiritual by-products. The Torah tells us, therefore, to live physical lives — eating, marrying, working, raising a family, etc. — *not as a concession to human nature*, but because that is precisely the means by which we fulfill our purpose here: converting earthly, physical human existence and experience into a series of heavenly acts (our "fruits"). We truly are "trees of the field."

The deeper lesson of the third day of creation, therefore, is that we are heavenly souls rooted in the earth for the purpose of transforming earth into heaven. As in heaven, so on earth. This lesson comes into clearer focus when we examine the verses describing the creation of Man.

The Fifth Element

The Creator developed the world in stages. He started with inanimate objects (second day), proceeded to vegetation (third day), then animal life (fifth and sixth day), and finally humans. (In Hebrew: *domaim, tzomayach, chai, medabar.*) In this scheme the human species is one of the components of creation, albeit the highest component. However, Rabbi Yehudah HaLevi, author of the classic, *Kuzari*, adds that there is a fifth element: *Yisroel oved Hashem*, "Israel who serves G–d."

The truth is that this fifth component is not really mentioned explicitly in the sixth day of creation, because Israel is not a fifth element *by right of their creation*. Rather G–d gave to humanity, the fourth element, the opportunity to promote itself into the fifth element. Nothing else in creation was given this opportunity. A mountain cannot raise itself to the next level — once a mountain always a mountain. The human being, by contrast, has the choice to make itself a higher level and become a true servant of G–d. Thus, G–d did not technically create the fifth element. He only created the *potential* to become such. That is why it is not stated outright in the verses.

"Making" Versus "Creating"

Although it is not stated directly it is unmistakably alluded to in the following verses:

> And G–d said, "Let us make man in our image, as our likeness; and let them have dominion over the fish of the sea, and over the birds of the sky, and over the cattle, and over all the earth, over all the creeping things that creep on the earth." (Genesis 1:26)

Then, in the next verse (1:27), the Torah adds:

> And G–d created the man in His image; in the image of G–d He created him; male and female He created them.

Why is the second verse necessary? What does it add? Analyzing the two verses, the initial difference is that the first verse uses the word "making," *na'aseh* ("Let us *make*") while the second uses "creating," *vayivra* ("and

[G–d] *created*"). There is a significant difference between "making" and "creating." To "make" means to use *what already exists* and bring it together into the formation of an object. To "create" means to bring something into existence *that did not exist previously*. The first verse, therefore — which talks about "making" man — speaks about the human being as a combination of *previously existing elements*. The second verse — where it talks about "creating" man — refers to the human being as *a creation, as something brand new*.

Another difference between the verses is that the first is in the plural: "Let *us* make man in *our* image, as *our* likeness." Who is G–d enjoining to help Him make man? According to *Ramban*[35] it is the earth. (I.e. "*our* image" refers to G–d *and* the earth.) The human being was made from the elements of the earth, elements which had earlier been created[36] and were now to be brought together in the "making" of Man. Accordingly, "in *our* image, as in *our* likeness" refers to G–d's "making" Man from the elements of the earth, which had previously been created. The second verse, by contrast, is singular: "And G–d created the man in *His* image. . ." Here G–d — and G–d alone — "creates" the man. The image is *exclusively* G–d's. It was not "made" in consonance with the earth or any other elements.

The Difference Expounded

Clearly, then, these two verses point to two different human potentials.[37] The first is the human being who is

SO ON EARTH

superior to but who ultimately shares features with the earthly, physical world. He was "made" by G–d *with* the earth. The second is the human being — *Yisroel* — who serves G–d. He was "created," not "made," because in essence he antedates the physical world and transcends it. He is not inherently part of the physical world. The servant of G–d cannot be limited to time or space; as a servant he is an extension of G–d and G–d is not limited to time or space.

Adam was given a choice who he wanted to be. His question was: How do I choose to identify myself? Am I creation — albeit a human being, the apex of creation — who is ultimately only part of the physical world? Or am I an extension of the Transcendent One? As the former I am a *creation* of G–d. As the latter I become a type of *creator* myself. After all, I was created on the fourth level. I can choose, however, to raise myself to the fifth. In so doing, *I create myself* into a new being. G–d did not per say create me on the fifth level. He only created the potential. *When I raise myself to the fifth level it is as if I create myself.*

The bottom line is that from the beginning the human being was created not only the most dominant creation, but with the potential to promote himself to a level whereby he transcends the label "creation," whereby he embodies the very stuff of the divine essence.

Different Orientations

What is the real difference between the fourth level creation and the fifth? Orientation, and specifically: orientation toward the physical. Is the physical world the end goal of creation or is there a higher purpose? The way we view the world makes all the difference. For instance, the first of the 613 commandments can be understood on two levels.

> And G–d blessed them [the man and woman] and G–d said to them: Be fruitful and multiply, and fill the entire world and subdue it. . . (Genesis 1:28)

On the strictly literal level G–d's commandment to "be fruitful and multiply" means to have children. And indeed G–d was telling all humanity that they should involve themselves in the process of perpetuating the species and inhabiting the entire globe. Included in this idea is the exhortation to have a good marriage, to build and maintain a healthy body, and to enjoy life.

That is only one level, though — and it is only the level intended for the human as a fourth level creation. To the human on the fifth level there is an additional meaning: be fruitful and multiply your *good deeds* and fill the earth with them. Our Sages teach that the true offspring of a righteous person are his righteous acts and good deeds.[38]

Of course, a fifth level creation also has to bear physical children. In *addition*, however, his acts transcend the physical; his physical acts produce spiritual offspring. And that is why the destiny of the righteous is resurrection.[39] His physical body has a spiritual counterpart which is destined for resurrection and existence in eternity.

SO ON EARTH

The same two levels of interpretation exist for the exhortation to "fill the world and subdue it." The fourth level human being interprets it to mean cultivating fields, building highways, domesticating animals, etc. To the fifth level human being it means "fill" in the earth with the contents of spirituality. In other words, when you eat food it is not only to give you strength to cultivate more fields, build more highways, domesticate more animals, etc. When you eat it is to give you strength to serve G–d; it is to give you the opportunity to fulfill the Divine Will. Whenever the fifth level human being is taking part in the mundane he is "filling it" with spirituality because his orientation is such.

The real difference, then, between the fourth level human being and the fifth is not necessarily the act itself, for *they are both expected to take part in the same earthly, mundane acts.* The difference is orientation. The fifth level human being lives a life not, at its root, in service of his own needs, but in the service of G–d's needs. That is what makes him a servant of G–d. He eats not really to satisfy his stomach or his desires. He eats ultimately because he wants to serve his Master, the Creator.

Living up to the Standard

Although this may sound like a simple difference it really is more difficult to carry out than it seems because oftentimes a person is tested. Often he has to make a choice between satisfying his own desires or forgoing his desires for the sake of carrying out G–d's will. He has to totally nullify

AS IN HEAVEN

his will before the will of G–d. And that is always a lot easier said than done.

It is so difficult in fact that it took 2,000 years before a human being demonstrated enough self-nullification to promote himself to the fifth level. Adam was not successful, as we know. He ate from the tree in direct opposition to G–d's will. Had he aligned himself to G–d's will he would have acquired the name *Yisroel oved Hashem*. (And, if so, everyone born from him — which in fact would have been humanity in its entirety — would have been called Israel.) Adam sinned, however, and it took 2,000 years before a person came along who proved absolutely that he was truly a servant of G–d.

That person was Abraham.

And that is why Abraham was tested ten times.[40] The tenth test, the most difficult of all, called on him to slaughter his son. That was the ultimate test because it showed he was even willing to nullify his legitimate spiritual desires before G–d's will.[41]

There were many righteous people who lived between Adam and Abraham, but they never sacrificed their all to acquire — permanently — the status as a fifth level of creation. They possessed the soul of a *potential* fifth level creation but had never fully *actualized* it, at least to the point where it fused permanently into their being. Abraham's success allowed him to establish a permanent level for his offspring. They became "naturalized citizens" of the fifth level. In essence, that higher potential, that higher soul —

SO ON EARTH

which had "floated" from descendant to descendant from the time of Adam — found a permanent resting place in Abraham's being.

This is why Abraham's offspring, after further purging and processing, were selected to receive the Torah. The Torah's 613 commandments ensure that the Jew orients his or her soul toward G–d's will. After all, such a code of laws represents (among other things) submission of personal desire to the Divine Will, sacrifice of certain aspects of the physical, etc. And that sacrifice identifies them as perpetuators of Abraham's ideal.

Jews are human beings like non-Jews, but they differ as a soldier differs from a civilian. All citizens of a given country are obligated to uphold certain laws no matter what their color, gender, or ethnic background. At the same time, every country has its army. Where do the soldiers come from? From volunteers. The moment you volunteer for the army you accept upon yourself stricter rules and regulations. A soldier can be put in military prison for the slightest infraction. As unfair as it may seem it makes sense. A soldier has to exhibit a greater degree of discipline because the safety of the country is dependent on the military.

Abraham was the first volunteer. His children, therefore, the Jewish People, became the army of G-d. G-d gave them special rules and responsibilities — as well as special privileges. As long as they obey the rules they deserve recognition for possessing a certain exalted stature in comparison to regular citizens. And this is not prejudice because

AS IN HEAVEN

anyone can join the "army" — as long as he or she is willing to pay the price, which means accepting a particular responsibility with a stricter code of rules and regulations.

Accepting upon oneself this Divinely bequeathed set of rules and regulations is the very thing which declares that one is an offspring of Abraham, the first one to totally nullify his personal will to the Divine Will. That earned him, and whoever is identified as his legitimate offspring, an actualized state of being above and beyond the original portion allotted Adam.

Partners vs. Employers

"My son, My firstborn is Israel." (Exodus 4:22)

G–d calls Israel His son. A child is the extension of the parent. The parent "conceives" him, brings him into the world, raises him, and sets him on the path of life to make his mark in the world. A firstborn is the most "choice" child, the ultimate representation of that which the parent truly stands for. If G–d, therefore, calls Israel His firstborn son, then Israel is the living representation of G–d's most primal expression, of G–d's first thought, so to speak.[42]

The nature of a person identified as Israel is highlighted by the teaching that a human being can aspire to become "a partner with G–d in the process of creation."[43] This statement is not exaggeration or allegory. It is meant literally and at minimum has the same repercussions as any human partnership, as it is defined in the code of Jewish law.

SO ON EARTH

That code — the *Shulchan Aruch* (*Choshen Mishpat*) — has many chapters on the laws of partnerships. From them we learn that a partner differs from an employee in several significant ways. For instance, according to Jewish law, if an employee sold merchandise worth $100 for only $50 his employer can nullify the entire transaction. An employee has no right to set a price not in agreement with the desires of his boss. Regarding a partner, on the other hand, the *Shulchan Aruch* says: *shutaf mah sh'aso aso*, "a partner — whatever he does is done." If your partner makes a foolish mistake selling merchandise worth $100 for $50 you cannot nullify the transaction. What was done was done.

The first difference between an employee and a partner, then, is that an employee's mistake does not ultimately affect the overall operation. "Whatever a partner does," on the other hand, "is done." His actions, for better or worse, change the business itself. *The same is true for the "business" called creation.* We are partners with G–d and our contribution to the partnership directly impacts upon the well-being or deterioration of the "business."

Another characteristic of a partner is that a partner is someone who by definition contributes something absolutely unique and vital which the other partner(s) cannot do. For instance, in business oftentimes you find the "salesman" type partner with the one who knows how to make the product. Or you find one partner with a talent for seeing the larger picture with another possessing the talent for accomplishing the nuts-and-bolts of the operation. Each partner is more to the other than just an employee. Each is a creative contributor of an absolutely vital function, a function without which the overall operation would falter.

The same is true for anyone who is a partner with G–d. Our contribution is a contribution which G–d on His own will not — indeed, "cannot" — do. (Of course, G–d can do anything. He, however, created the world in such a way where He *voluntarily* limited Himself to a certain extent. He did so in order to give His potential partners an opportunity to make their own vital contribution. He left a place undone where only His partner can get the job done. It is indeed possible, therefore, for a human being to do something G–d Himself "cannot" do.) This, in essence, is the idea of becoming a partner with G–d.

Adam's Choice

This also explains the essential choice Adam was given: to be an employee or a partner. Every human being, at the minimum, is responsible to see himself as an "employee" of G–d whose job is to take part in the development of creation. Above and beyond that, however, every human being has the chance to voluntarily promote himself into partner status. And that was the choice Adam was given. He was created an "employee." He was given the opportunity, though, to promote himself into a "partner." Of course, he did not take advantage of this opportunity, as we will explain in detail later (Chapter 13).

SO ON EARTH

Although Adam lost the opportunity, the human race did not irrevocably lose its opportunity thanks to the efforts of Abraham. He earned, not only for himself but for his progeny, the Jewish People, the status of a permanent partnership with G–d. A Jew is a born partner with G–d, for better or for worse. The Gentile of course has a purpose here, a very necessary purpose. And he receives reward, this-worldly and next-wordly, for good work. (He even receives bonuses for exceptional work.) However, he is an employee. He has the option to promote himself into partner status, if he is willing to pay the price, but unless he does so he remains an employee.

A Jew, on the other hand, is a partner — whether he likes it or not. He is the son, the firstborn son of the "Boss," and has inherited a partnership in the "business." His efforts, therefore, directly impact upon the operation of the "business" of creation. And consequently his performance is not weighed as the employee's performance is weighed. The Jew shares directly in the profits, and, similarly, is responsible for the losses. In the end, though, partner status is an advantage. There is no higher ideal to strive for.

In conclusion, then, Abraham fulfilled the potential (as represented by the second verse, 1:27) given Adam. He is the true Adam, the Adam that Adam himself never became.[44] And that is why the Sages say that for his sake the entire world was worth creating (see Chapter 8). He was the human being G–d really had in mind, so to speak, when He created the universe.

CHAPTER 6

Soul Mates

- *Explaining the idea of marriage, giving and taking, the connection between the animals passing before Adam and the "building" of the woman, the meaning of becoming one flesh, the curses, and how they serve as vehicles for fulfillment in marriage.*

The Torah idea of marriage can be summarized as follows: The purpose of marriage is not only to bring children into the world, which is an important independent requirement in and of itself. It is also to allow human beings the opportunity to exercise the divine image (*tzelem Elokim*) in which they were created. This is signified by the verse:

> And G–d created the man in His image; in the image of G–d (*tzelem Elokim*) He created him; male and female He created them. (Genesis 1:27)

The qualities of "male and female" are mentioned *only* in this verse — the verse discussing the "image of G–d" — because the ultimate goal of a man and woman uniting as

SO ON EARTH

one — i.e. getting married — is to give expression to the divine image (*tzelem Elokim*). It is a goal unto itself. How exactly, though, is the divine image expressed specifically through the marital union? This needs explanation.

Givers and Recipients

Why did G–d create the world? As best as we can understand it, "The nature of good is to bestow good." G–d is the ultimate Good and therefore He wanted to bestow goodness. Consequently, He created a recipient for His good. We, humanity, are the recipient. It is our "job" to receive and accept G–d's goodness.

If G–d is good, and the nature of good is to bestow good, it follows then that the nature of the divine image *in the human being* is to bestow good. And this indeed is the root of the human instinct — indeed, the human need — to give. **Giving is in reality a reflection of our innate divinity.** We want to give because the divine image[45] within each of us is aching to express its nature.

If G–d's "dilemma" is to find a recipient to receive His goodness, then our dilemma — as beings made in His image — is to find a recipient for *our* goodness. This explains why when Adam was "alone" this status was designated "not good."[46] The reason is because *he did not have a recipient to receive his goodness.* He had no one to make him into a giver.

"The world was built for kindness (*chessed*)."[47] The purpose of creation is to allow for the possibility of one entity

AS IN HEAVEN

to bestow kindness on another. Nowhere is this potential more poignantly expressed than in the love between a husband and a wife. That makes marriage, in its highest sense, *the* forum for giving vent to the divine image latent in each of our souls.

The Maximum Desire

> And *Hashem*/G-d said, "It is not good for the man to be alone; I will make him a help opposing him." And out of the ground *Hashem*/G-d formed every animal of the field, and every bird of the air; and brought them to the man to see what he would call them .... But for the man there was not found a help opposing him. And *Hashem*/G-d caused a deep sleep to fall upon the man, and he slept. And He took one of his sides ... and built it into a woman; and He brought her to the man. And the man said, "This time bone of my bone, flesh of my flesh." (Genesis 2:18-23)

The optimal relationship is when both husband and wife have the maximum desire for each other: he has the maximum desire to give, and she has the maximum desire to receive. This, in fact, was G-d's design in the otherwise enigmatic act of bringing the animals to pass before Adam. What does giving the animal names have to do with anything? And why does the Torah mention it in the middle of the description of the creation of Adam's mate? The answer is that by passing all the animals before him Adam came to realize how alone he was in the world, that there was no creature like him. He truly knew what it meant to say: "It is not good for man to be alone."

SO ON EARTH

Why did G–d do that to Adam? To make him depressed? To make him lonely? No. Rather, G–d's plan was to create in Adam the *yearning* for a mate like him. Only after G–d caused all the animals to pass before Adam, therefore, did He "cause him [Adam] to fall into a deep sleep" and make his wife. The reason was because only then was his feeling of aloneness and loneliness at its height. And, consequently, only at that point was he ready to be introduced to his soul-mate.

There is another nuance here as well. Today we hear of lonely people showing exceptional kindness to a pet: a dog, cat, fish, bird — even a rock. This strikes us as odd or even tragic when the pet is the only thing in such a person's life. What is the real tragedy? Because these people want to satisfy their innate desire to give — their divine image — with a receiver who cannot maximally appreciate it. *The giver feels satisfaction only to the degree the receiver is capable of appreciating the gift.* If the recipient is incapable of appreciating the gift to the degree that the giver is capable of giving it — that is sad. If a human being's divine image is being used for nothing more than animals (or rocks) — that is a tragedy.

When G–d caused the animals of creation to pass before Adam he tried to utilize his ability to give on them. He tried to give to the duck; he tried to give to the cow; he tried to give to the monkey. And so on. In each case Adam was ultimately unsatisfied because no animal could fully appreciate the total extent of his ability to give. Therefore, only after seeing how all the animals could not fulfill him was it possible for Adam to fully appreciate that Chava (Eve) was his completion; she was his partner, the only one for whom his deep-seated urge to give was meant.

To Become One

> Therefore a man leaves his father and mother and cleaves to his wife for them to become one flesh. (Genesis 2:24)

G–d originally created the human soul as a composite of the male and female qualities ("... male and female He created them"). Picture your brain and heart. Even though one can make the distinction between the two, nevertheless in the final analysis both are part of a single individual. It would sound ridiculous to say your brain envies your heart; or your heart feels jealous towards your brain. They are one.

So, too, a man and a woman. Even before they were born they were distinct, the man possessing unique qualities in some ways and the woman in other ways. Yet, they perfectly complemented each other. They existed in a perfect giver-receiver relationship.

If so, why did G–d tamper with this natural harmony and "build" a separate body for Chava into which He cast the female portion of the soul? The answer is that as long as the giver-receiver parts — the male-female — were one entity there was really no great accomplishment in giving and receiving. G–d therefore separated them. By separating the

SO ON EARTH

female from the male He made one side "opposing" the other. As two *physically* separate individuals it would not be such a simple matter for them to give and receive naturally from each other. Each would have a physical, materialist, ego-centric nature to overcome. There would be real opposition to the otherwise natural expression of their divine image and their inherent unity. G–d did it, in other words, to create the opposition.

This is also why the emphasis is on becoming one *flesh*. ("Therefore a man leaves his father and mother and cleaves to his wife for them to become one *flesh*.") In a soul sense a man and a woman are one. However, in a bodily sense — in "flesh" — they are two. The "flesh" is naturally predisposed toward ego-centricity, competitiveness, jealousy, etc. That is why the goal is specifically to become one *flesh*. If they learn to cooperate with each other as one flesh, then they will naturally experience the primordial state of being one soul. If they do not, then even if they are true "soul-mates" in the fullest sense of the term their marriage will not necessarily be smooth or happy.

A "soul-mate" means that the other person is a *spiritually* ideal complement to you. Living with a soul-mate, however, does not mean to say that there will not be a lot of work to do. There will be. That special feeling of "soul-oneness" a couple feels cannot be accessed as long as they are two "fleshes," however. Oneness in marriage does not result from the *natural* complementary predisposition of the two parties — although that can help — but from the

AS IN HEAVEN

work of quelling the inherent self-centeredness, competitiveness, etc. that is synonymous with the physical body. That is why a husband and wife are exhorted to become one *flesh*. In soul terms they are naturally one; in "flesh" terms they have a lot of work to do.

A successful marriage begins, then, with a particular orientation. The first question cannot be: "What will I get out of it?" Rather it must be: "What can I give in it"? If each is worried about taking care of the needs of the other they will find fulfillment. Such a marriage improves over time, unlike many marriages today. In order to become one each partner has to first be tolerant of and sensitive to the other's needs. Then they have to find satisfying, acceptable ways of helping each other fill his or her own needs.

The Woman's Curse and the Man's Curse: Helping Each Other Overcome

In addition to serving as a framework for satisfying the spiritual needs of a person, marriage is a vehicle for satisfying the deepest emotional needs of a person. These emotional needs can best be explained in the context of verses which take place after the sin.

After the sin, Adam and Chava were cursed:

> To the woman He said, "I will greatly multiply your pain of childbirth; in pain you shall bring forth children; and to your husband will be your desire, and he shall rule over you." (Genesis 3:16)

SO ON EARTH

By the way, the statement "and he shall rule over you" does not mean that a husband is to act like a dictator toward his wife. What is means, simply, is that she will be dependent upon him. As citizens are dependent upon their ruler, so too the woman will be dependent upon her husband (and shortly we will explain the root nature of this dependence).

And to the man He said, "Because you listened to the voice of your wife and ate from the tree which I commanded you, saying, 'Do not eat from it,' cursed is the ground for your sake. In pain you shall eat of it all the days of your life; thorns and thistles it shall bring forth for you. And you shall eat the herb of the field. By the sweat of your brow you shall eat bread until you return to the ground from which you were taken, for you are dust and to dust you shall return." (3:17-19)

Man and woman were cursed with two distinct curses. This is important to know because one of the functions of marriage is to help alleviate, or at least compensate, for each other's curse. The man, who does not go through the pain of childbirth, must support his wife during her suffering. The woman, who is not cursed to work "by the sweat of [her] brow," can give her husband the necessary encouragement in his working-earning life.

Let us analyze this. The woman's pain of bearing children is not limited to the labor pains at birth. It includes the stormy moods her bodily cycle puts her through each month. A woman's body chemistry takes her regularly through highs and lows men do not experience, and can never fully appreciate. This is one of the things which makes her dependent on her husband. Her moods make her hyper-sensitive to her husband's feelings toward her.

Obviously, then, it is in the man's hands to give her the assurances she needs. He does not go through terrible emotional peaks and valleys every month. He tends to be more steady. The ability to alleviate her curse is therefore in his hands. That is why our Sages are so careful to exhort a man to be extra-sensitive to his wife's needs. (For example: "[A man should treat] his wife like his own body and honor her more than his own body...."[48]) Following their advice is the antidote which helps alleviate the woman's curse.

In a similar vein, the man's curse can be compensated for by the wife. The man is cursed to work "by the sweat of his brow." In a deeper sense this means that the man's ego will be continually challenged because he is the one who has to venture forth into the world to put bread on the table. The possibility of coming home empty-handed is a deep, continuous source of fear and worry. *Bitachon*, or "faith" in G–d, is his constant test.

Women, on the other hand, were not given this curse. Therefore, they can have more serenity; they can display more natural trust in G–d. Deep down a woman knows that her primary responsibility is not to put bread on the table. To alleviate the man's curse it is therefore very important for a wife to always encourage her husband, to stroke his ego, and supply him with words of comfort and *bitachon*: "It's not the end of the world. G–d provides the food for our table. And if we don't have money, at least we have our health." And so on. The woman's sensitivity toward her husband is her readiness to always say a kind word of encouragement which will relieve him of at least some of his worry.

A well-functioning marriage displays these dynamics: the man softening the woman's curse, the woman the man's. Unfortunately, today, society indoctrinates women to compete with men in the workplace. While this is considered progress in the general society, in actuality it is just the reverse. It is not enough that the woman has her curse. Now she wants the man's, too!

This of course increases the woman's pain. In her drive for "equality" she does nothing but gain a double portion of curse. Moreover, concentrating as she is on her full-time career she is less likely to be able to perform her part in the alleviation of the man's curse. She ends up shortchanging herself and her marriage.

The Torah outlook does not deny that situations exist where the woman can and should work, and an observant couple consults with their Rabbi in all circumstances. However, even when an observant woman works full-time outside the home it is not for the same reasons as those of the women in general society. Her priorities are straight. Establishing a home in alignment with Torah values is paramount.

In any event, the curses that the man and woman received were not punishments or retributions in the normal sense.

AS IN HEAVEN

Marriage is a working dynamic. Each partner has special qualities that were meant to be used in service of the other. This is what helps create the emotional bond between them. Without each other the individual is not really capable of alleviating his or her own curse. Therefore, while the curses did create greater difficulties for all involved, they were also vehicles for (re)creating the bond which makes marriage a bastion for blessing and emotional wholeness.

In Summation

Marriage is an institution designed to satisfy the physical, emotional, and spiritual needs of both the man and the woman. G–d created one soul with male and female principles, and encased each principle in separate male and female bodies. In doing so, He set up a situation where the human being not only finds multiple forms of fulfillment but can actually emulate the divine.

As in heaven, so on earth.

In its highest sense marriage is the act of imitating G–d as a bestower of goodness onto another. And that is what it means to be made in the divine image.

CHAPTER 7

And It Was Very Good

- *Explaining the problem with calling creation "very good," the twelve stages of Adam's creation, why the ability to sin is a gift, a profound explanation of the word "meod," and why the baal teshuva holds a special status.*

At the conclusion of the sixth day G–d reviewed everything and concluded that it was "very good." In the previous days G–d only mentions that it was "good." What on the sixth day made it "very" good? To understand the answer at its depth we must analyze a passage in the Talmud.

The Twelve Hours

Rabbi Yochanan bar Hanina said: The [sixth] day consisted of twelve hours. In the first hour, his [Adam's] dust was gathered; in the second he was kneaded into a shapeless mass; in the third his limbs were shaped; in the fourth he was infused with life; in the fifth he arose and stood on his

And It Was Very Good 125

AS IN HEAVEN

feet; in the sixth he gave the animals their names; in the seventh he was paired with Chava; in the eighth they ascended to bed as two and descended as four; in the ninth he was commanded not to eat from the tree; in the tenth he transgressed; in the eleventh he was put on trial; in the twelfth he was expelled.[49]

From the above, we learn that Adam's creation took place in twelve stages. In the first, G–d so to speak skimmed the dust off the surface of the earth and used it to make the substance of Adam. In the second, the dust was "kneaded" like a piece of clay. In the third, Adam's limbs were "pulled out" and formed from the clay. In the fourth, his body was given life. In the fifth he stood on his feet.

In the sixth hour Adam called all the animals names. The name-calling was not just giving meaningless labels, however. It was reflective of Adam's knowledge of the root meaning of every creature. The Hebrew name of every animal is not just a label, but a "DNA code" expressing the essence of the creature, its place and purpose in creation. If Adam could give the animals their names that means he understood creation as an architect understands a building he has seen the blueprint of. Torah is the blueprint of creation. Adam saw creation at its root, which is the Torah.

The sixth hour, then, was truly monumental. In it Adam received the soul power necessary to perceive the Torah. Despite that, however, as the Torah says, Adam was still "not good" (as he is referred to in 2:18 — man "alone," i.e. without a mate[50]). Consequently, in the seventh hour, G–d put Adam to sleep and "built" Chava (Eve) from one of his

SO ON EARTH

sides. Essentially G–d divided Adam's body into two unique halves and infused a portion of the original single soul into each half.

In the eighth hour they gave birth to Cain and Abel (and their twin sisters, as the Talmud teaches[51]). In the ninth hour G–d put them in the idyllic world of the Garden of Eden and commanded them not to eat from the Tree of Knowledge. In the tenth hour, they disobeyed G–d and ate from the tree. In the eleventh hour they were put on trial (G–d said, "Where are you?"). And finally in the twelfth hour they were thrown out of the Garden.

Now, when you think about this passage it presents a great difficulty. The Torah states that after G–d purveyed everything He did on the sixth day He concluded that it was "very good." However, as we have just learned, in the very hour He was stating that everything was "very good" — in the twelfth hour — Adam and Chava were driven out of the Garden! How then could G–d call everything "very good" if at that moment Adam, the purpose of creation, was getting expelled from paradise?!

Teshuva

The answer is explained by the Maharal.[52] He derives from the above that *sin was no less a part of Adam's creation than anything else which happened during the twelve hours of his creation. The possibility of sin is part of the perfect plan*; in fact it is what truly catapulted creation into the status of "very good." Without it we would never have

AS IN HEAVEN

had the opportunity to do *teshuva* ("repentance" or "return"). Thus, the statement that G–d saw how everything was "very good" is, ultimately, a reference to giving man the ability to do *teshuva*.

This needs further explanation, however. The way we normally understand it a person does something wrong and then does *teshuva* to correct the wrong. *Teshuva* is the means to an end. In this perspective the best thing is to never have sinned, in which case it would never have been necessary to do *teshuva*. If so, however, how can it be accorded the status of "very good"? It would have been better if Adam had never sinned to begin with!

The truth is that *teshuva* is not only a means. Looked at from another angle it is an end goal in itself. Our Sages tell us, for instance, that "in the place that a *baal teshuva* stands not even the perfectly righteous (*tzaddikim gemurim*) can stand."[53] Sin, in this perspective, is a *vehicle* for *teshuva* because it enables a person to attain a higher level than one who never sinned.

If this idea sounds strange, imagine the following scenario. Two men became millionaires. One man, however, lost all the money through his own foolishness. Nevertheless, eventually he learned from his mistakes, went back into business, struggled very hard for a long time, made some sound investments, and eventually made back his million.

These two men both now possess a million dollars. Who is happier, though? The second millionaire is happier. The

SO ON EARTH

first is happy, too, of course, but all has is a million dollars. The second person not only has the money, but *himself*; he regained his loss. And that is what the Sages mean when they say a genuine *baal teshuva* commands a certain status that is greater than the perfectly righteous person, the person who never really sinned to begin with. The *baal teshuva* knows what it means to be thrown out of paradise; he knows what it means to suffer in the darkness and isolation of exile; he knows what it means to be confused and fragmented. He has the accomplishment of overcoming his loss as well as an appreciation of what he now possesses. His status is thus not merely good, but *very* good.

If Adam had never been given the ability to sin he would have forever remained "good," as all the other elements in creation are called. He would have been a passive recipient of the "good" in a world in which he was created and found himself. Once, however, Adam was created with the potential to sink lower than the original level of creation he was given the concomitant ability to slingshot himself above the original level ("good") to the level of "very good"; he was given the opportunity to not only experience the good but say he earned it for himself.

This idea can be seen in a deeply profound way by analyzing the letters of the Hebrew word for "very": *meod*. *Meod* is spelled *mem-alef-dalet*. These are the same letters (though in a different order) that make up the name "Adam" or "man" (*alef-dalet-mem*). When Adam sinned and became "mixed up," he got his priorities all out of order. His original state, *alef-dalet-mem* (Adam), became corrupted into *mem-alef-dalet* (*meod*).[54] That was a sin.[55] The overall situation, however, was "very good," because his sin gave him the chance to correct the order — to restore himself to the status of "Adam," *alef-dalet-mem* — and regain himself. That truly made creation *very* good.

No Reason To Despair

Without the potential to be expelled from the Garden we would never have the opportunity to bring about, *of our own doing,* our "return" to the Garden of Eden. The elevated status of a *baal teshuva* would not be possible without sin. This also helps explain why Scripture lays down a principle that, "There is no righteous man upon the earth who does good and sins not."[56] Sin is practically an unavoidable component of life. (That does not give one license to sin, of course. To sin with the intention of doing *teshuva* afterward is totally unacceptable, as the Sages of the *Mishnah* teach.[57] Rather, **we must do our utmost to avoid sin**. The verse merely informs us that the best efforts of even the most righteous people cannot fully prevent absolute avoidance of sin.) Sin is built into life. Why? Did G–d have no choice? Did He do something wrong or overlook something? No! It was an intentional design to allow the possibility of *teshuva*, which is an end goal itself.

And this is also why the Sages say: "What was *very* good about the sixth day? The evil inclination (*yetzer hara*)."[58] *Falling into the clutches of the evil inclination is something*

SO ON EARTH

we must avoid at all costs. However, G–d created His world in such a way that sin is virtually unavoidable even despite one's best efforts. Therefore, there is no reason for the person laden with sin to despair. G–d, from His perspective, labels that situation "very good." He knows that sin opens the door to the greatest good: the ability of a person to come back *on his own* and thereby earn his rightful place in paradise. This is "very good."

Part IV

PARADISE

CHAPTER 8

Verse Of Transition

- *Explaining Genesis 2:4, the transition this verse signifies, the reason why it uses two names of G–d, and the unmistakable allusion it contains.*

"These are the products (*toldos*) of the heaven and the earth when they were created (*biheebaram*) in the day Hashem/G–d made earth and heaven." (Genesis 2:4)

This verse signifies a transition. Prior we have been given a sketchy overview of creation. Now we are about to go back and focus in upon some details of one feature in creation — the main feature: Adam-man. This verse then is an introduction to a new direction of the Torah narrative.

As part of the introduction the word "products" (of heaven and earth) is used. "Products" is a good translation for *toldos*, which is often translated "generations" or "offspring," because what is about to follow is not so much a

AS IN HEAVEN

genealogy as a description of the "by-products" or results of human actions.

The previous verses recounting the six days of creation mention in a general way those things which were essentially *G–d's* "production." The purpose of this verse (2:4) is to introduce us specifically to the "by-products" of heaven *and earth*, i.e. the results from the *human* contribution to the great production of creation. Thus, the narrative to follow details the life of Adam in the Garden of Eden, his fall, and all the ensuing events of biblical history. These are the most significant human contributions, for better and worse, which have had the greatest impact on the overall process of bringing to fruition the original potential of creation.

Hashem Elokim

The first most noticeable feature of our verse is the name of G–d which is used. In fact, it uses two names together: *Hashem* (the four letter name of G–d) and *Elokim*. Until now the narrative had only used the latter.

The Torah does not employ any of the several particular names of G–d without reason. Generally, each name refers to a different aspect of G–d. *Elokim* refers to G–d who set up the natural laws of the universe, for instance. Its numerical value is equivalent to the numerical value of the Hebrew word for "nature."[59] *Elokim* is therefore G–d in the aspect of limiting Himself within nature.

The name *Hashem,* on the other hand, is not so much an aspect of G–d, but the name most representing G–d's

SO ON EARTH

essence. It is a combination of the Hebrew words "is, was, and will be."[60] *Hashem* refers to "G–d who perpetually recreates the world." He did not just create it once long ago, but each and every moment exists only because He wills it to exist each and every moment. (See Chapter 3.)

The question now arises why the Torah decided to use *Hashem-Elokim* here in our verse after the basic six days of creation have been described. Why didn't it use it beforehand? Furthermore, if two names of G–d were to be used why is the order *Hashem-Elokim*? After all, the Torah had been using *Elokim* all along. Now that the name *Hashem* is introduced shouldn't it come after *Elokim*?

The answer is that the name *Hashem* is not only higher than *Elokim* but *Hashem* preceded and even made possible, so to speak, *Elokim*. (See Supplement, "The Creation Of Elokim.") That is why it was mentioned first of the two names.

Why is the name *Hashem-Elokim* specifically mentioned here, though: in the verse following the initial description of the six days of creation? The answer is because G–d in the aspect of *Elokim* is all that was necessary to technically create the world. Now, however, from our verse on, the text is going to redescribe the creation of man — specifically the infusion of his higher soul (2:7). And man is not exclusively a creation limited like everything else created during the six days; he is not the exclusive product of *Elokim*. Man, as we will learn, has an aspect of *Hashem* within him; he has the potential to transcend mere creation, as we

AS IN HEAVEN

explained in Chapter 5. For that it is appropriate for the Torah to not only mention G–d in the aspect of *Elokim*, but G–d in the aspect of *Hashem* as well.

For the Sake of Abraham

These few words of verse four, then, really signify something monumental. First they teach that from the beginning creation was intended to create "products" (i.e. *toldos*). Next, we learn that these "products" would not be mere expressions of the knowable G–d's (*Elokim*) will, but would also somehow express G–d's most transcendent, most creative, and most unrestricted aspects (*Hashem*). Finally, this verse also contains a clear and specific allusion to that creation who came to embody the very purpose of heaven and earth: Abraham.

> These are the products (*toldos*) of the heaven and the earth <u>when they were created (*biheebaram*)</u> in the day *Hashem*/G-d made earth and heaven. (Genesis 2:4)

As the *Midrash*[61] comments:

> "When they were created" — *biheebaram*. Rabbi Yehoshua ben Korchah said, *biheebaram* is identical in lettering with *b'Abraham*,[62] to teach us that [all was created] for the sake of Abraham.)

The verse can thus be read:

138 *Chapter 8*

SO ON EARTH

"These are the products (*toldos*) of the heaven and the earth — Abraham . . ."

Abraham, the one who came to truly express the transcendent aspect of *Hashem*, is the central "product" heaven and earth produced. For his sake they were created. Adam had been given the opportunity to fulfill the highest ideal of creation, to promote himself to the fifth level of creation, as we explained previously (Chapter 5). But he and no one after him did so — until Abraham. Abraham regained the stature lost by Adam. And therefore this verse makes an unmistakable allusion to him.

This verse of transition, then — this verse which foreshadows the creation of Adam and the great potential given him — tells us that even as Adam was about to sin and lose his potential, nevertheless heaven and earth harbored within them the person capable of recapturing and fulfilling that lost potential — Abraham.

CHAPTER 9

The Essence Of Prayer

- *Explaining Genesis 2:5-6, the reason rain did not fall immediately, the importance of prayer, the great machinery of creation, self-centeredness, and the need for gratitude.*

And no growth of the field was yet on the earth; plus no grass of the field had yet sprouted, for *Hashem*/G–d had not yet caused it to rain on the earth and there was no man to work the earth. (Genesis 2:5)

The Torah's style is to follow through on one lesson all the way before retracing its steps and detailing a tangent within that lesson. After providing a general outline of the six days of creation, this verse returns back to the sixth day *before* the creation of Adam, yet after G–d had finished everything else. On the sixth day basic plant life existed in potential but had not yet "sprouted." As Rashi explains

SO ON EARTH

none of it had yet *emerged* from the surface of the earth.[63] It awaited the rain. The rain, though, also awaited something:

> The reason He [G–d] had not caused it to rain was because there was "no man to work the earth," and no one to recognize the value of rain. But when Adam was created he recognized and knew the importance of rain. He therefore prayed and the vegetation began sprouting. (Rashi)

Adam was created a fully intelligent human being whose mind grasped the root knowledge of the entire universe. The instant he became aware that he was alive he had the ability to appreciate everything, including the value of rain. And that is what G–d was waiting for: for a part of His creation to recognize the value of rain and pray for it.

The question is why did G–d wait? Why did He create a world where He "had to wait" for man in order to bring the rain? And how, really, is rain dependent upon man? These questions need examination.

A World of Kindness

Olam chessed yiboneh, "The world was created for loving-kindness."[64] As best as we can understand it, the reason G–d created the world was to have a recipient upon whom to bestow kindness.[65] Human beings are the intended recipients of this kindness[66] and therefore the tool whereby G–d can fulfill His purpose in creation. *We are not just passive recipients, however.* We "trigger" G–d's kindness, and in so doing allow Him to give.

The Essence Of Prayer 141

AS IN HEAVEN

How do we trigger G–d's kindness? In a word: acknowledgment. If we first long for something and *then* get it, we truly appreciate it.

When G–d created heaven He instilled it with every potential that we could possibly want or need: life, food, shelter, children, good times, etc. Every spiritual and physical thing a person needs from the day he is born till the day he dies is stored away in heaven, so to speak. However, in order to activate these potentials — in order to have them "rain down from heaven" — a condition must be met: the person has to want it in the first place; he has to be aware of his need and acknowledge his dependence upon G–d as the ultimate source of all blessing.

When we acknowledge G–d as the source we not only open the storehouses of heavenly blessing, but actually give G–d "pleasure," if it were possible to say so. For G–d's "pleasure," and the reason He created us, is to make us happy. The more we acknowledge and respond happily to His gifts, therefore, the more we fulfill His desire. If, on the other hand, we are numb to G–d's kindness or refuse to acknowledge that He is the source of these gifts, then we diminish or stop up the flow of heavenly blessing.

Creation is one great system. It is an enormous machine set in motion with its rich treasures waiting to be utilized. Nothing happens, however, until there is an initial need. Therefore, even though G–d had finished creation He kept its true wealth locked up in potential until a recipient who could properly appreciate the wealth was created. Adam

SO ON EARTH

was that creation. He was the trigger for the world's spiritual and physical abundance.

An Awakening From Below

And this idea is confirmed by a nuance in verse 6:

> And a mist *arose* from the earth and watered the entire face of the ground.

After Adam recognized the necessity for rain he prayed and it fell. Technically speaking, however, it did not *fall*. Rather a mist *"came up"* from the ground. The deeper implication is to teach that *we must first do something down here to trigger a response from above*. That is the symbolism of the rising mist. It represents what is called an "awakening from below." The mist which arose from the ground is symbolic of the fact that human initiative below is the agent of eliciting heavenly response above.

Flipping the Switch

The question is: What does human initiative, the "awakening from below," translate itself into? What is the main vehicle through which a human being expresses this all-important acknowledgment of G–d's blessing?

The answer is prayer — heartfelt, sincere prayer.

A heartfelt prayer means that a person acknowledges he is in a position of need and that that need can ultimately only be fulfilled by G–d. Prayer, therefore, is the pre-

AS IN HEAVEN

condition to blessing. It creates (or confirms) the giver-receiver relationship between G–d and man.

The act of prayer is like flipping an electrical switch. The electricity in your house's outlets is ready to flow through the wires. Giant transformers and electrical generators at the local power plant are continually generating enormous amounts of electricity. Yet, there will be no light in your home unless you actively go over to the switch and flip it on.

This is prayer.

All the blessings of heaven we need to complete our tasks here on earth are stored in their heavenly chambers, pulsing with their life-giving energies, ready to rain down upon us. It is up to us to pull the switch, however: which means to pray, because prayer is our way of acknowledging our dependence upon the Giver of Blessings.

There are many types of "switches." Some bring life. Some bring health. Some bring wealth. Some bring peace in the world. Some bring redemption. And so on. There are so many things we as individuals and we as members of the greater world community need. None of it can be accomplished, however, without pulling the appropriate switches, without a real heartfelt cry, without prayer.

Working Out the Inner Person

Our Sages tell us that "work" (*avodah*) is a euphemism for prayer. Prayer is the "work" of the heart,[67] the inner person. When we preface our needs with prayers to G–d we do

SO ON EARTH

Him the greatest favor: we establish our awareness as receivers and thereby make His pleasure as a giver, if words could express it, possible. When a person prays, therefore, he "works" for and earns G–d's blessing.

Seen in this light now, the verse: "And there was no man to work (*l'avod* as in *avodah*) the earth," takes on a deeper meaning. It means that there was no man to do the "work of prayer." The earth was dry and barren because prayer is needed for G–d to rain down blessing and before Adam prayer had never been uttered, the value of rain had never been appreciated.

On another level, the "earth" is a symbol for the human personality. Indeed, the first human was called "Adam" because his parts were taken from the "earth" (*adamah*). The statement that the earth was barren and untilled means that the human personality was barren and untilled. How does one bring to fruition the hidden life dormant in the human personality? Through work. But what type of work is required? The work of the heart: prayer.

Self-Centeredness and its Remedy

If prayer is the "work of the heart" it is by no means easy work. From the moment we are born we are inculcated with the idea that we deserve everything. A newborn receives his mother's milk which is produced especially for him. He grows into an infant whose slightest cry is responded to by his caretakers. He advances to toddlerhood where everyone dotes over him. And so on. From the moment we are born

AS IN HEAVEN

we are trained to believe that our needs will be automatically met when we desire. Part of the process of maturation, however, entails outgrowing this inbred tendency. A person who never grows beyond this stage is handicapped by his own self-centeredness.

The Maharal, commenting on our verse, writes: "It is *prohibited* to perform a kindness for someone who will not appreciate the favor." Giving something to someone incapable of appreciation is prohibited because it will corrupt him further; *it will only make him more self-centered* because his problem is that he thinks he deserves everything anyway. A self-centered person does not even have the ability to be thankful. His prayers, if he prays at all, do not really affect anything significant. And the worst part is that the inability to be thankful robs G–d of His "pleasure," which is to give blessing and abundance to His creations. A self-centered, arrogant, person incapable of expressing thanks frustrates the entire purpose of creation.

G–d has compassion for all, though. How, then, does He deal with a person who has become insensitive to and takes for granted the great gifts he has been graced with? One way is that G–d will try to educate the person by taking away everything.

> Two friends were walking down the street when one of them mentioned to the other how his bank had "put him back on his feet."
> "Yeah? How did they do that?"
> "They repossessed my car. Now I walk all over the place."

SO ON EARTH

Sometimes G–d will "repossess" everything from us. This is a way of educating us to become more sincere human beings. By falling into the straits of despair a person will find it in his heart to really pray, perhaps for the first time in his life. Finally, when this person gets something back he will be thankful like never before.

We forget and take it for granted, but simply the opportunity to breathe air is a kindness of G–d. Every breath we take is something worthy of our thanks and praise to Him. We rarely think about it, but the privilege of simply being alive is truly something to be happy and grateful for.

If a person loses his job and becomes sick he will pray and pray and pray. One day, miraculously, he starts feeling better and his health is restored. Yet, because he has no income his entire focus is on praying to G–d for it. He has to be careful, therefore, that he not forget the lesson of gratitude. As much as he has a right and even an obligation to ask for money, nevertheless if he does so without first acknowledging *that which he has already received* he may end up accomplishing little. A person in such a situation first has to express appreciation for that which he received. He has to wake up in the morning and say, "Thank G–d that I am alive, that I am healthy, that my children are healthy, that I can keep the Torah." And then, afterward, he should say, "Oh, G–d, I need some money . . ."

Therefore, it is important to remember that before we open our mouths to ask G–d to fulfill our needs we must express our appreciation for what we already have. List all the good things you already possess and make sure to thank G–d for them. Chances are when you stop focusing exclusively on your need you will find it coming to you anyway.

On the other hand, when we fail to focus on what we have, or worse, when we focus on what we do not have, we feel bitter. Those emotions close the heart. And if you want to access the hidden storehouses of blessing locked up in heaven you need an open heart flowing with gratitude. Nothing grows without first a heartfelt prayer.

The Great Machinery of Heaven and Earth

Our verse (2:5), then, teaches a very relevant and powerful lesson. Until the time alluded to in it creation was a great potential, an incomprehensibly great machine surging with energy and power. Nevertheless, it was nothing more than a potential. It had not yet been fully activated because humans had not yet been created. "There was no man to work the earth," which means there was no man around to pray to G–d and thereby acknowledge his dependence on heaven. But then Adam was created and began the hard work of prayer and gratitude.

And we are still involved in this work today. We are extensions of Adam. To this day we are all still tilling the soil of our souls in the attempt to sprout forth the blessings of heaven and earth latent within.

CHAPTER 10

Soul Searching

- *Explaining the verse where G–d blew into Adam a soul (Genesis 2:7), life after death, the idea of two souls, the shofar, the human identity crisis, the mid-life crisis, and the number one question we must all ask ourselves.*

About a century ago, an international conference was held in Vienna, Austria, to address the question: Is there life after death? Upon hearing of the conference topic, a famous rabbi laughed.
"What do you find so funny?"
"Are they so sure there is life *before* death?"

Is there really life *before* death? "Yes, of course," you answer. We are alive.

But who is the "we"? Who are you? Who am I? Am I my body, my feelings, my memory? Take a heart transplant patient. When he says "me," who is he referring to? Whose heart is pounding with excitement? Who is doing the feeling? Some scientists have even conjectured about the possibility of brain transplants. Who would be doing the

AS IN HEAVEN

thinking in such a transplant? We can picture a man with Mr. Jones' heart, Mr. Smith's brain, Mr. Jefferson's kidney, Mr. Washington's skin, Mr. Franklin's blood, etc. — all in addition to his body.

Who, then, is the "me"?

As much as modern civilization has advanced, it has not answered that question. In so doing, it has only strengthened it. The essence and substance of who we are is as tantalizingly elusive as ever before.

The Plane and the Pilot

Of course, the Torah is not elusive when it comes to identifying the essence and substance of the human being:

> "And G-d . . . breathed into his [Adam's] nostrils an eternal soul [literally, the breath of life]." (Genesis 2:7)

The body is a vehicle for the soul. It is like an airplane. An airplane does not fly for its own sake, but to bring people from one location to another. So, too, the body. The soul "boards" it at birth, and "disembarks" it at death. It is the soul which is the essential substance of a human being, and the body which is merely the vehicle.

The Tenth Saying

As explained earlier (Chapter 2), the world was created with Ten Sayings.[68] The original Saying — *beraishis* — was infused with such high degrees of "G–dliness" that

SO ON EARTH

creation was not able to contain it in its raw form. It therefore needed to be "transformed" downward into levels suitable for creation. The object created with the tenth Saying contained the least potent "voltage" of G–dliness; it was the farthest removed from the Divine.

That object, the tenth Saying, was the human being.

A human being is composed of the darkest matter. We are the farthest from G–d in the sense that we have the potential to deny G–d. (See Chapter 2.) At the same time, paradoxically, G–d gave us the potential to become the highest element of creation, in fact to transcend creation: He gave us the eternal soul.

> And *Hashem*/G–d formed (*vayeetzer*)[69] the human of the dust of the ground, and breathed into his nostrils an eternal soul. And the human became an alive being. (Genesis 2:7)

"G–d formed the human of the dust of the ground" — i.e. the human was created from the earthly part, the part sharing much in common with the animals — "and breathed into his nostrils an everlasting soul [or "breath" of life]." The mystical books remark that one who breathes into another gives into him something of his own essence.[70] Through that act of blowing, therefore, G–d actually instilled a part of Himself into the physical human; He instilled into us the "soul of [eternal] life."

The human *body*, therefore, was created from the tenth of the Ten Sayings. That is why it is a very dark, physical thing, capable of becoming a Hitler and doing all types of despicable acts. At the same time, however, we were bestowed with a soul. The *soul* was not given us in the same way the body was. It was not bestowed via the act of speech (i.e. through one of the Ten *Sayings*), but in the most ethereal way — through an act of blowing: "And G–d *blew* into him an everlasting soul." (Note that the verse does not say, "And G–d *said*, I will blow the everlasting soul [into Adam]." It simply says, "And G–d blew . . .") He "blew" into the original human being a part of Himself. Blowing is an act which transcends words; it represents the idea that G–d actually put an aspect of His inner self into the human being.

A human being, consequently, is the combination of two elements: the finite body and the transcendent, divine soul (*neshama*). The reason for creating us with this dual nature can best be understood by very briefly explaining the idea behind blowing the *shofar* on Rosh HaShannah (the day commemorating the creation of Adam).

We are made of two opposite parts. The physical part was made with the tenth Saying. The spiritual part (the divine soul) was not made with any Saying. It was simply "blown" into us. The idea of the Rosh HaShannah service is to declare to our Maker (as well as ourselves) that we identify with our divine part. This is accomplished with the *blowing* of the *shofar*.

"Blowing" a *shofar* is an act which imitates the original act of G–d's "blowing" an aspect of His divinity into us. On Rosh HaShannah, therefore, we blow the *shofar* to

SO ON EARTH

demonstrate that we identify *not* with the product of the tenth Saying (the body), but with the pure, divine soul.

Citizenship

This is a vitally important point to understand, so let me illustrate it with the following analogy: A person who wants to venture into space needs a spaceship. The function of the spaceship is to protect the astronaut by reproducing the environment of his place of origin. Conversely, imagine a creature who could only survive in space. To survive on earth he would need an "earthship." He needs his original environment built into his "earthship."

So, too, the world. There are actually two worlds: heaven and earth. The two are connected, however, through the human being. A person is made of a body, which eventually dies, and a transcendent soul, which is eternal. Our body is the "citizen of earth," while our divine soul is the "citizen of space." The human being is a combination of these two "citizens." And the number one question in life is: *to which are you committed — the body or the soul? To which citizenship do you ascribe?*

And you can only be a citizen of one or the other. Yes, with your protective covering you can venture into both — a physically oriented person can experience spirituality, and a spiritually oriented person can experience physicality — but where are you at home? And life is a never-ending challenge to not only believe in our hearts that *we are citizens of heaven temporarily stationed on earth*, but to actualize

AS IN HEAVEN

that feeling in our everyday lives, in every nuance of our everyday lives, through our everyday actions.

Of course life continually challenges us to identify with the pull of the body. You want to read meaningful books, but the newspaper is much more convenient and less of a strain. You want to save your money to give more to needy causes, but you have an urge to spend it on relative trivialities. You want to identify with the divine image, the hidden light, the truly infinite part of yourself which is above time and space. But you find yourself as if magnetically drawn toward the shadow part, that finite part of yourself which exists only within time and space.

This is the inherent dichotomy of being human. We all have an enormous identity crisis. We do not know who we are. Animals do not have identity crises. Physical matter is not conflicted over its true nature. We are different, however. By our very natures we are confused. And our body in many ways has been given the upper hand in this struggle. Nevertheless, we also have a divine soul which can become a tangible part of our lives if we live a life which caters to *its* needs, if we identify ourselves as a citizen of *its* laws.

That is never easy. The desires of the body and the desires of the soul are often contradictory. What one likes the other does not like, and vice-versa. Yet, that is the ongoing conflict each of us feels within. In fact, if we do not feel that conflict something may really be wrong. We may be so numb to our soul's desires that we cease to feel them.

SO ON EARTH

Nevertheless, the real you — the you you were put here to identify with — is your divine soul. And life is the opportunity to forgo your natural identification with the body in order to identify with the desires of the divine soul.

The Womb or the Tomb

The Sages teach: "At forty, a man gains wisdom."[71] Why at forty? Can't a person become wise and educated at a much earlier age? The answer is that at forty the powers of the human body begin to wane. A person's orientation toward the physical, therefore, begins to diminish. The fantasy that he is going to conquer the world, or that he is going to be famous, or that he is going to acquire certain possessions are recognized as such: fantasies. (Or in the rare cases where these fantasies are more or less realized he begins to wonder if they were really everything he had made them out to be.) He now knows that he is on the other side of life, going downward.

If he is a reflective person — and even if he is not to a degree — this fact cannot help but impinge upon his consciousness. Suddenly, all those philosophical ideas he heard in his youth, which he thought were so irrelevant at the time, start creeping forward into his mind. He was intelligent when he was twenty and thirty, but he was too preoccupied with the pursuit of his fantasies, whatever they were, to really pay attention. He brushed statements about the meaning of life under the table.

At forty, though, the undeniable waning of his physical powers changes his entire mental framework. He starts thinking about what he has really accomplished in life, what is really important to him, what will happen to him when he leaves the world. He is not necessarily more intelligent, but he is open to wisdom in ways he was not capable of being open to before. That is why only first, "At forty, a man gains wisdom."

Time Versus Eternity

It is not always pleasant, but awareness of entry into midlife is always sobering. And if one stares the sobering truth squarely in the eyes he may be able to turn crisis into bliss; he may be able to grow in the second half of life in ways he never dreamed possible beforehand.

"The length of our years are seventy; and if we are strong, eighty . . ." (Psalms 90:10)

Look at your watch. See the seconds tick away. Those seconds will never return. Time's incessant march will leave in its wake only death: the death of a past that will never come again.

A materialistic person does not live for seventy or eighty years — he *dies* for seventy or eighty years.

At the same time, each of us has a soul. And that soul originates from — and at some level will always remain connected to — the realm of the G–dly, a realm above materialism, above time, above these seventy or eighty years of death. The divine soul is our connection to eternal life, to perpetual birth.

Our Sages tell us that this life is a corridor to the next life.[72] Just as emergence from the womb constitutes corporeal birth, detachment from the body is the birth of the soul. Just as the seven, eight, or nine months in the womb are the period of gestation preceding earthly birth, so, too, the seventy, eighty, or ninety years on earth are the gestation period preceding heavenly birth.

Life is a womb for the soul. Like a womb its value is not what it is but rather what it brings into existence. If it brings into existence the seed of eternity, if it nourishes and nurtures the impregnated egg of the G–dly, then it is truly life. If, on the other hand, it exists for itself and is hollowed of anything other than the walls of its own temporary existence, then it cannot really be called life. It is only a vestibule of death. A tomb for dust and ashes.

How do you view your life? There is probably no single more important question you can ask yourself because the way you answer it will perforce have the greatest possible repercussions. Are your seventy or eighty years an end unto themselves? Or are they a gestation period for a future birth? Are they a path to the grave or a doorway to infinity?

This is a scary question to think about but it is a basic question each of us must ask. Am I congruent to the needs of my higher, divine self or am I a prisoner to the call of my body? Who am I? Whether you are observant or not these

AS IN HEAVEN

are questions everyone has to seriously think about once in a while at least. Life, in every sense of the word, may hinge upon it.

CHAPTER 11

The Garden Of Eden

- *Explaining the verses concerning the Garden of Eden, the intimate relationship between this world and the next world, a perspective on suffering, and the meaning of living the moment.*

And *Hashem*/G-d planted a garden east in Eden; and there He put the man whom He formed. (Genesis 2:8)

The Garden of Eden is synonymous with eternity. That is why it was planted, *m'kedem*, which is usually translated "to the east." *M'kedem*, however, also has the connotation of "original" or "primordial." The meaning therefore would be that Garden of Eden (Eden means "pleasure") is a primordial place. It is a realm before time, a "time" of timeless time.

Just as the divine soul is the eternal part of the human being (see the previous chapter), the Garden of Eden is the

AS IN HEAVEN

eternal part of the globe: it is the soul of the world. That may help explain why a soul which earns heavenly reward is said to pass on from this world *into the Garden of Eden*. It is returning to its home, and that is its reward.

What we tend to forget or may not even be aware of is that the Garden of Eden was originally not meant to just be the place of *other-wordly* reward. It was "planted" on this earth and had Adam not sinned the entire world would have become a Garden of Eden. And indeed that is the goal of present history: to return to the point where Adam sinned and from there, like the four rivers which went out of the Garden, spread it to the entire world.

We make the mistake, therefore, when we think dualistically, i.e. that there are two absolutely unconnected worlds: *olam hazeh*, "this world," and *olam habah*, the "World To Come" (i.e. the Afterlife). There is really only one world. It is just that this world has not yet evolved into the Garden of Eden it is destined to become.

We are also mistaken, therefore, when we think, simply, that people worthy of heavenly reward leave one world and go into the next like a person who leaves one apartment to go into another. When the Sabbath comes, do you move into another dwelling? Do you switch locations? No, you take the Sabbath on in the same house or apartment you lived in during the week. Yet, if it is a properly run Jewish home that same dwelling is transformed. It has taken on the aura of Sabbath. The garbage — both physical and spiritual — is thrown out. (Hopefully both types are taken out

SO ON EARTH

during the week as well.) The best tablecloth is out. The best utensils are out. Everything is white. You did not move away. You did not change the air. Rather, you took the domain where you lived a whole week and turned it into a Sabbath.

This world is like a weekday leading into the everlasting Sabbath. One day it is going to become the next world, *olam habah*. The way you train yourself to experience this life is the way you will experience the afterlife . . . except there the experience will be much more pure and heightened. But the basic experience is the same; your basic personality here is your basic personality there.

In this sense, then, there really is only one world: this world. However, this world is going to one day become the next world, the World To Come, the Garden of Eden.[73] If you want the afterlife to be a Garden of Eden experience, then you have to learn in which ways the present life possesses elements of a Garden of Eden-like experience.

Living Now

Sometimes people give up on life. They say, "I cannot be happy in this life. I hope that in the next world I will have a better life." They rationalize that as long as they are suffering here they are going to be worthy to get *olam habah*, the World To Come.

That is mistaken thinking.

You cannot really develop *olam habah* if you do not have *olam hazeh*. While there is no avoiding pain, and it is

The Garden Of Eden 161

AS IN HEAVEN

natural to not like it, nevertheless painful life situations have their own worth. Indeed, knowing that what you are going through here somehow holds a key to enhance your *olam habah* can electrify your ability to enjoy and experience life *now*. Suffering must not be an excuse for stagnation and despair. If you do nothing in *olam hazeh* what will you have in *olam habah*? Therefore, a person must find strength to do whatever he or she can do even in the midst of hardship.

How can a person be happy amidst suffering? The answer is by realizing that every second of this life contains within it the seed of *olam habah*. The truth is that a little accomplished amidst hardship is usually more than a lot accomplished during times of ease. Every experience in this life — including difficult times — is the nuclear power source for the pleasure you will reap in the life to come. Knowing that, a person can learn to radiate an inner tranquillity and contentment even during difficult times.

Every Moment has its Gem

Every moment has its gem — even moments (or lifetimes) of pain and suffering. And everyone's life has been specially arranged so that billions of moments, each with its unique response, have been laid out to be experienced and decided upon. Yet, it is up to the individual to discover the value of every moment. And no one else can make that discovery for you. It remains an undiscovered gem if you do not take responsibility for uncovering it.

SO ON EARTH

Each of us has to constantly ask: What is NOW giving me? Every moment of life is a jewel. If you do not seek to discover the meaning and mission of this moment, what are you doing? Now is the moment to accomplish, because if you do not utilize NOW, when will you have the moment again? It will never come back.

A certain holy Jew used to wake up every morning and say to himself, "Good morning and welcome twenty-first of *Iyar* (or whatever date on the calendar it was). What a great day! We have been waiting since the beginning of creation for you. We waited for you so long, and yet now time is so short. I will only be with you for the next twenty-four hours. After that, I will never see you again. Therefore, let me get started. I promise that I will live with you every second."

This is the attitude we need to optimize our time.

On the other hand, it must be pointed out that even an entire lifetime of wasted moments can be recaptured. Every element of our past can be turned around for good. The idea is to make a choice of such deep and far ranging quality that it returns one to one's original status as a soul, as an entity made in the divine image.

The wonderful thing about writing on a computer with a word processor is that you do not have to fear mistakes. Before computers, if you made a mistake you had to use white-out and possibly even retype the entire paper. Today, you simply go back to the point of the mistake, correct it, and the word processor reorganizes the entire page for you.

The same is true with our spiritual mistakes. The past is never completely lost as long as we are alive. In a single, emotionally-packed, deeply-felt moment anyone can "return" to his original status as a citizen of the soul. And when we do, we correct all our past failings. Like entering a correction into a document on the computer, one moment of "return" can send ripples of change through all the other moments of our life already passed.

It may not be easy. But the truth is that such a change can happen in a moment. The real you is the soul-you and that soul-you hungers for truth. People get depressed because they fail to identify themselves with their eternal souls. To "return" means to become once again the real you — the soul-you which can only tolerate so much lethargy and self-deception. When you failed in the past, that was not you. The real you is the "you" you discover in a moment of naked, sober truth. Such a moment is almost sure to be painful, yet when you uncover — rediscover — your real self you find a part of yourself you can love eternal, and there is no greater pleasure than that.

Spirituality is not about fortune-telling, communication with spirits, or the like. Spirituality is about living the moment. A true sourcebook of spirituality tells us how to live now . . . this moment we are all part of.

CHAPTER 12

The Tree Of Life

- *Explaining the Tree of Life as it exists today, the real meaning of freedom, why our world is like Tiffany's, and what it means to "Choose life!"*

And out of the ground *Hashem*/G-d made grow every tree that is pleasant to the eyes and good for food; the tree of life also in the middle of the garden.... (Genesis 2:9)

[Torah] is a tree of life to those who grab hold of her. (Proverbs 3:18)

The Torah is called a tree of life. It is the tree of life *"in the middle of the garden..."* That means it is literally the root of this world.

Picture this. You are canoeing down a fast-water river. All of a sudden you are thrown into the surging rapids. Cut loose from the security of the boat you are out of control and in danger of drowning. Suddenly, while tossing and turning in the waters, you look up and see a tree. You grab for it and hold on with dear life.

AS IN HEAVEN

This is like life.

Life is a continuous flow of everchanging, surging currents. Fads, philosophies, finances, leaders and governments are in constant flux. Nothing in this world has permanence. The success with which we meet change and adversity is dependent on how true and well-rooted our beliefs are.

Torah is a "tree of life to those who grab hold of her." That tree is the inner truth of life which does not change. It stands in the middle while the waters of the modern, mundane world rush all about. There are other things in the water which may at first appear to be able to save us from drowning, but when we grab onto them in our moment of need we find out that they were nothing other than dead wood or shallowly-rooted trees.

No outlook in the long record of human civilization has weathered the ebb and flow of history like Torah. It is not just another philosophy, psychology or self-help trend; and it is not just another religion. It is the root of this world, and what you gain by grabbing onto it is not just some transient happiness — you gain life, real life.

Of course, by Torah we mean more than Bible stories. Torah is the inner truth of the Creator. The Creator expressed this inner truth in the form of Hebrew letters and words called the Five Books of Moses. These five books — and their explanation, the Oral Torah — contain the values and way of life G–d designed for humanity, which would be reflective of that inner truth.

SO ON EARTH

Torah is not just a vaguely defined call to morality and spirituality. Many people want to be moral and spiritual, but their pursuit of these ideals is limited to what they can discern with their own finite, human understanding. And sooner or later the shortcomings of these idealistic-sounding yet mutable, man-made definitions of morality and spirituality become evident to all.

Torah, on the other hand, is G–d's infinite understanding given to Moses on Mount Sinai in both the written form and the interpretation of the written form: the Talmud or oral Torah. Taken together, the Torah above all is the divinely-prescribed guidelines for living; it is a clearly defined lifestyle based on the 613 commandments. These commandments produce a very definite pattern of life. They are the skeletal structure around which the inner intent and soul of the Torah come to fruition.

The Torah therefore is the tree of life incarnate. The lifestyle it prescribes holds the key to transforming the experience of temporal life into the experience of eternal life.

Give Me Freedom or Give Me Death

A common complaint, especially from people raised in a secular environment, is that even accepting the argument that the Torah is truly a divine teaching documenting a lifestyle bequeathed the world by G–d — even so, they cannot possibly see themselves living the 613 commandments. The modern person is used to freedom. She considers it an inalienable right. How could a person ever be happy giving it up even for a divinely ordained lifestyle?

The answer is that the truly free person is one who lives the Torah.[74] The reason is because the type of freedom that really counts is not mere political freedom — i.e. liberty — but freedom of the spirit. Modern democracies, at best, provide only liberty. And liberty, indeed, is something to be valued. However, in the final analysis liberty entails having merely certain basic *external* rights. Freedom, on the other hand, is an internal state of being, and it is an internal state achieved, paradoxically, through the restricting — actually "harnessing" — of one's focus. (That explains why even in a society which affords the maximum liberty there will always be people who feel a continual and otherwise ill-defined sense of frustration and imprisonment. The society emphasizes liberty, not freedom.)

In its very restrictiveness Torah is a freedom-producing path. To illustrate this clearly, imagine the following scenario.

Grabbing Diamonds

Imagine a person was told he could go into the vault at Tiffany's and had one hour to grab all the gems he wanted. The hour begins, but since there is so much time, and he knows that he could grab more than he would ever need in half that time, he decides to let himself take in the sights for just a few moments.

SO ON EARTH

Mirrored displays, majestic fountains, gourmet food, amusements, interesting people, etc. — there are so many beautiful sights all around that he quickly loses himself in them. A half-hour goes by. Forty minutes. Fifty minutes. Fifty-five. Fifty-nine minutes go by, and all of a sudden he remembers: The hour, it's almost up! As the sixtieth minute strikes, he sees a gem lying around and grabs it.

He leaves the store, goes to the jeweler next door, and asks how much it is worth.

"You want to sell this?" the jeweler says excitedly, gawking at the stone.

"Yes."

"I'll give you $100,000 for it."

Let me ask you: How will this person react: happy or sad? At first he may be happy, however afterwards regret will sink in. "Was I out of my mind? If in one moment I grabbed $100,000, in one hour I could have grabbed millions and millions of dollars worth of stones!"

Our world is a Tiffany's. It possesses rare gems — elements of eternity — amidst a Disneyworld of temporary temptations and distractions, which although possessing their own momentary beauty only serve to draw one away from the real opportunity of grabbing diamonds, of grabbing our stake in eternity.

Creation is not an end in itself; it is a means. This life is a vehicle for us to transport ourselves from a framework of time into the experience of eternity, from the realm of the physical to the realm of the G–dly. However, it is easy to get distracted and detoured; it is easy to become a prisoner of time.

Freedom to walk into a prison is not freedom — it is an abuse of freedom. If we abuse our freedom and attach ourselves to things of an exclusively physical, temporary nature, we become chained and addicted to them — we lose the freedom to complete the very purpose for which we were placed here. Therefore, the restrictions of Torah are actually the mechanisms of freedom. They help us unshackle ourselves. They help us use our time to grab diamonds.

Returning to the illustration of our friend who was given the opportunity to enter the vault in Tiffany's: Imagine beforehand that he was forewarned how he would be tempted with things which would distract him from grabbing the gems. To counteract the distractions, however, he was told that he would be given a list of "dos and don'ts" which he was told he should follow *no matter what*. These instructions would keep him focused on the task at hand and thereby ensure that he would leave with enough wealth to buy his own Tiffany's.

Beforehand, he may have dismissed the necessity of the instructions. Now, in retrospect, after he blew his chance, he will appreciate the significance of the list of "dos and don'ts." They would have freed him from becoming entangled with the distractions. They would have freed him by telling him how to optimally use every moment of his

SO ON EARTH

precious time there. All he had to do was follow the instructions.

This is the Torah. It helps us avoid getting hopelessly entangled in the temporary and steers us to the elements of eternity present in this temporary life. It is our list of instructions, telling us where we should go and where not to go, what we should do and what we should not do, how we should do it and how we should not do it. Every moment possesses the choice of time or eternity, and the Torah is our guide for choosing eternity.

Consider the act of eating, for instance. You can eat to fill your stomach, which is basically the same reason animals eat, or you can turn your eating into a G–dly act by following the commandments the Creator gave you about eating. In the first case, you used your time to eat; in the second, you used it to gain eternity. Similarly, you can work, make a lot of money, and consider yourself self-made, or you can make your money and contemplate the help from Above, without which your seeming success would have never materialized.[75] In the former, your time is literally money — nothing less and nothing more; in the latter, your money bought you a deeper awareness of G–d and thus helped you cash in time for eternity.

Likewise, you can indulge in your natural urge for intimacy and become self-centered or you can marry, enjoy life with your spouse as the Torah prescribes, and change your orientation to one who is genuinely selfless.[76] In the former, your time of enjoyment lasted one night, one year, several years, but nothing more; in the latter, your time produced not only enjoyment but eternity.

Eat, but know what to eat, how to eat, and why you are eating. Make a lot of money, but know how you are allowed to go about making money, what to do with it once you have it, and what the true goal of making money is. Marry and enjoy your relationship, but know the how, when, and why of your relationship. Every thing, every moment can be used.

The Torah is not an idealistic, abstract philosophy. It is not a vague call to love. It is a way of life which seeks to help us convert the matter of the mundane elements from our everyday, worldly life into the spiritual energy of eternity. Each commandment, in its own way, teaches us how to make G–d a reality in our lives, to bring Him out from behind the murky shadows, and turn physical living into a tangible expression of spirituality, to turn earthly life into a heavenly life.

Life — this life — is potentially a Garden of Eden. It is beautiful, and even those things of temporary beauty can be used as tools to attain eternity. However, it is not possible to do so without the "instructions for eternity" bequeathed to humanity by the Eternal G–d.

Choose Life!

"I put before you life and death, blessing and curse — choose life!" (Deuteronomy 30:19)

SO ON EARTH

Notice, the Torah does not exhort us in the negative: "Don't choose death." It is worded positively: "Choose life!" The reason is because remaining as we were born — just living our physical, finite existence without any boundaries or direction — leads naturally to death. And therefore death is not a choice; it is the natural outcome of our physical existence if we do not actively grab life.

"Choosing life" means actively making the choice to discover and convert the eternity — the spiritual diamonds — of our very temporary temporal lives. By telling us specifically what to refrain from and what to partake of — and how to partake of it — the Torah teaches us how to really live. It is not a restriction. It is a life preserver. It helps us stay afloat and then teaches us how to swim beyond the horizon of our physical, time-bound lives.

Part V

CIVILIZATION UNFOLDS

CHAPTER 13

Adam's Sin

- *Explaining the verses of Adam's sin, the temptation, the lessons we need to learn from his failure, a guideline for distinguishing between the evil inclination and the good one, a way to protect yourself from sin, the difference between a humane act and a G–dly act, the need to be conscious, and the difference between "duties of the limbs" and "duties of the heart."*

And *Hashem*/G–d took the man, and put him into the Garden of Eden to watch it and to keep it. And *Hashem*/G–d commanded the man, saying: "Of every tree of the garden you may freely eat; but of the tree of knowledge of good and evil you shall not eat, for on the day that you eat of it you will surely die." (Genesis 2:15-18)

It is a mistake to think that Adam's sin was simple or without calculations. To the contrary, he thought about it very deeply, had the most profound reasons for doing it, and generally understood what he was doing. Indeed, Adam had not only the highest reasons but the holiest rationales for eating from the tree.[77] His test, though, was one of the

AS IN HEAVEN

most difficult tests imaginable, one that we still fail repeatedly to this day.

Dismantling the Jigsaw Puzzle

We have discussed (Introduction) how in the original scheme earth was a mirror image of heaven. Into this heavenly earth Adam was created. He opened his eyes and saw a world which teemed with the spiritual; the earth was as beautiful as heaven.... Excluding one slight but important difference: the earth had the *potential* to become shattered.

If heaven is a beautiful painting, then earth is the same painting but on the face of a jigsaw puzzle (as we described in the Introduction). The earth Adam first saw was a "jigsaw puzzle" still in its original, whole form — it was not yet broken up. In that state is was virtually impossible to tell the "jigsaw puzzle" (earth) from the original, whole painting (heaven). As a jigsaw puzzle, however, it had the potential to be dismantled. It came whole in "cellophane" wrapping, so to speak, and a "red pull-thread" with instructions warning: DO NOT PULL THIS THREAD, OTHERWISE THE PUZZLE WILL FALL OUT AND COME APART.

This was Adam's situation. G–d showed him the earth in its entirety and told him it was his. He could satisfy himself with everything in it — with one exception: the tree of knowledge of good and evil. "On the day you eat from it," he was told, "you will surely die." In other words, G–d was telling him that if he ate from the tree the "entire puzzle

SO ON EARTH

would fall apart." Death would be brought into the world; the earth would cease to be an ordered creation mirroring the symmetry of heaven.

Adam reasoned to himself something as follows: "G–d warned me not to eat from this tree. Why would He warn me, though? It is like the 'red thread.' If someone put it there it was obviously meant to be pulled." (Did you ever see a "Wet Paint!" sign and next to it a freshly painted wall with fingerprints in the paint?)

Adam reasoned, "What could be the advantage of pulling the thread? If I pull it (read: if I eat from the forbidden tree) the earth will become chaotic. But that must be exactly what G–d wants, for if I have the potential to create the chaos then I must also have the potential to restore order."[78] And if I restore the order — if I rebuild the jigsaw puzzle myself — then I will become a partner with G–d in creation. Therefore, G–d must want me to sin so that I get the opportunity do *teshuva*,[79] correct my wrong, and rebuild creation with my efforts."

Adam was absolutely correct in thinking that G–d intentionally put the "red thread" — i.e. the potential for sin, destruction — in the Garden of Eden. However, since G–d said, "Don't pull it" (read: "Don't eat from the tree of knowledge") he should not have pulled it *no matter what*. Why did G–d make it, then? That is G–d's business, not mine, Adam should have reasoned.

Although there was a real logic to his thinking he should have forgone the logic. *His test was to make human reasoning subservient to the word of G–d.* In so doing, he would have attained everything, including partnership. But he was too smart for his own good.

And this is a very relevant lesson to us today.

The Evil Inclination in Front and Behind

Each of us is a piece of Adam. And each of us has been assigned a piece in the great puzzle of creation to put back into its right place. We are here to restore our part and become a worthy partner with G–d in the process of creation. This is how we take part in the great process of restoring the world to its original grandeur.

The means to do so, however, *is by following G–d's will.* The best calculations, philosophies, and reasons are nothing compared to G–d's word. If they conflict with G–d's direct order, then the human being has to accept that and surrender his judgment to G–d's.

This, in my opinion, is one of the great challenges facing us today. And it is not only a challenge for people on the outskirts of Torah observance. Even the Torah observant Jew, who in principle wants nothing but to surrender himself to G–d, has to be careful to avoid dictating his own agenda.

Everyday in our prayers we ask G–d to protect us from the "*Yetzer hara* [evil inclination] in front of us and behind us." The evil inclination "in front of us" represents obvious misbehavior; it is the inclination to do things which are clearly wrong. What, though, is the evil inclination "behind

SO ON EARTH

us"? It is the inclination to do things which are not so clearly wrong. We have to be on guard against both.

Each of us on our own is so subjective that we cannot be sure that even our so-called good desires are truly correct. A person can even desire to become *more* observant for the wrong reasons. Of course, oftentimes a person should intensify adherence to detailed observance, however our inherent subjectivity can even distort us to act overly religious or pious.

Is there a way for a person on his own to tell whether the desire he feels is from the good inclination or from the bad? Usually, the good inclination never makes things easy; it rarely if ever "pushes." For instance, at the beginning the evil inclination tells you, "Don't take any time to learn Torah. Don't increase your commitment to observance." And so on. But you overcome. You make important breakthroughs. Then the evil inclination changes its tune: "Take on more. Do more. Become more religious than you can handle." He pushes the person to the other extreme.

A general rule is that the good inclination does not push. It's path is usually not the easy path. Maybe the right thing is to learn full-time now. But maybe not. Maybe the right thing is to intensify your observance or suggest it to a nonobservant person. But maybe not.

How can a person confronted with an important decision discern the objective truth? The answer is: "Make a Rabbi for yourself."[80] Torah is the conduit of G–d's knowledge. That is why *a true Torah scholar is the most important*

AS IN HEAVEN

person in the entire world. Such a person not only possesses academic knowledge but knows human inclinations, specifically the good inclination — the *yetzer tov* — and the bad inclination — the *yetzer hara*. No one like a *genuine* Torah scholar can deftly navigate the constantly shifting waters of the human personality.

In all circumstances a person must seek out an objective party. While theoretically that person can be anyone who knows you well, there is no one better trained in objectivity and the arguments of the *yetzer hara* than an *authentic* Torah scholar. Therefore, each of us has an obligation to seek out such advisors, to make ourselves know to them, so that we are not left to our own devices, which are almost always assured to give ascendancy to the enticing arguments of the *yetzer hara*, be they "in front of us" or "behind us."

And the World Came Tumbling Down

G–d created the tree of knowledge. If Adam was told not to eat from it, then he should have realized that the knowledge the tree bestowed was not of primary importance for him. What was of primary importance was to surrender his judgment to G–d's. But he didn't. That was his mistake. And we have been making the same mistake ever since.

Of course, Adam — like us when we rationalize our incongruence to the Divine Will — had a good reason. The best and holiest reason, in fact. He saw a beautiful world and a tree of knowledge which could have enabled him to become a partner with G–d in creation. "I know," Adam

SO ON EARTH

reasoned, "that if I eat from it I will bring destruction to the world, but eventually I will be able to rebuild it; and when I do I will fulfill the highest goal of creation: becoming a partner with G–d."

Adam's reasoning was flawless — except for one fact. G–d said, "Do not eat from that tree!" His test was to cast aside his holy rationales because in comparison to G–d's will they meant nothing. Knowledge is a handmaiden to will. And therefore there is nothing higher or holier than the Creator's will. According to a widely disseminated teaching of the *Arizal*, had Adam refrained from eating of the tree of knowledge that fateful first Friday afternoon of creation he would have been allowed to eat from it at the onset of the Sabbath anyway. But he didn't refrain. He ate prematurely.

And the world came tumbling down. The puzzle fell apart.

And we are still picking up the pieces.

Protection from Sin?

> And *Hashem*/G–d commanded the man, saying: "Of every tree of the garden you may freely eat; but of the tree of knowledge of good and evil you shall not eat, for on the day you eat of it you will surely die." (Genesis 2:16-17)

One of the great difficulties with the entire episode of Adam's sin is that we have a principle that a person who is totally absorbed in performing a commandment will be protected.[81] Total immersion in the good deed protects one from doing any sin. If so, how was Adam capable of sinning?[82] If we assume he was living with the highest level of consciousness, then we must assume he was continually immersed in the performance of a commandment. Consequently, how did he come to sin?

The answer[83] is that protection from evil only applies if you are *conscious* that you are doing the commandment, i.e. only if you are doing the act *because it is a commandment*. If, for instance, you help your neighbor unload his packages exclusively because your heart compels you to, you may be a nice person but your act is not a conscious fulfillment of the Divine Will. And in that sense it is lacking. While such an act may be laudable it does not protect one from evil.

On the other hand, one who acts with the consciousness that he is acting because G–d commanded him is surrounded by an aura of protection. His very consciousness that what he is doing is a commandment connects him totally to G–d. When one is connected to G–d his acts become much more than mere *humane* acts. They become *G–dly* acts as well.

This was exactly Adam's problem: he was not fully conscious that his mere act of eating was the fulfillment of G–d's will. That lack of consciousness betrayed the fact that he was eating for his own enjoyment. There is nothing wrong per say with eating for one's own enjoyment, but it does not create an aura of Divine protection. And that is why Adam was open to the challenge of the snake.

SO ON EARTH

Ochal Tochal

If Adam's downfall resulted from his failure to have the proper G–d-consciousness in his acts, where do we see this in the verses? Regarding all the trees in the Garden G–d said, *ochal tochal*, literally: "Eat, you shall eat." This double expression can be understood in one of two ways:

1) as a commandment (you *must* eat)
2) an invitation (you *may freely* eat).

The interpretation was left open for Adam. If Adam had understood the statement as a commandment, then in effect he would have been living in the Garden under two commandments: a negative commandment not to eat from the tree of knowledge and a positive commandment to "eat" (*ochal tochal*) from all the other trees. And, if so, consequently every act of eating from the permitted trees in the Garden would actually have been a conscious fulfillment of G–d's will (i.e. a positive commandment). Unfortunately, Adam understood G–d's words *ochal tochal* to mean that he was "free" to eat from all the trees. He was not, therefore, conscious that his eating was a fulfillment of G–d's will. The proof is in the snake's conversation with his wife Chava.

First, it should be mentioned that the snake in the Garden of Eden was not just an ordinary snake. In actuality it was the manifestation of a principle — the principle that the human being must be tested in order to earn his stature.

🍇 AS IN HEAVEN

Toward that end G–d created an angel whose express purpose was to confront Adam with challenging tests. The angel chose one creature through whom to perform its purposes. This was the snake. The original snake was a manifestation, then, of the heavenly representative of evil.

"And the snake was smarter than all the beasts of the field which *Hashem*/G–d made." (Genesis 3:1)

Since it was created for the express purpose of countering Adam, a being with almost divine intelligence, the snake was created with exceptional intelligence as well. And it knew that it could not perpetrate any evil against Adam if he was totally immersed in performing G–d's will. Therefore, before doing anything it had to probe to see if Adam had a weak spot.

"Is it true," the snake asked the woman, "that G–d said you are not permitted to eat from any tree of the garden?"

She responded, "We may eat [*nochal*] of the trees of the garden, but [not from the tree of knowledge]."

Her response betrayed her attitude. If she had interpreted G–d's statement of *"ochal tochal"* as a commandment she would have responded: "We were *commanded* to eat of the trees of the garden. . ." rather than "We *may* eat of the trees of the garden. . ." If that was her response, then the evil designs of the snake would never have been able to have been carried out. But she answered, "We *may* eat. . ." This revealed that she and her mate had not acquired the perpetual G–d-consciousness that protects one from evil. To them

186 *Chapter 13*

SO ON EARTH

eating was enjoyment, not the fulfillment of a commandment. The snake had its opening.

Duties of the Limbs, Duties of the Heart

The same test is placed before us today. There are 613 commandments. These are called the "duties of the limbs" because they primarily involve some type of physical action: we put on *tefillin*, we pray, we give charity, etc. However, strictly speaking the "duties of the limbs" do not cover most of our daily lives. In fact, some are only applicable when the Temple stands, or only at infrequent times, or only to kings, etc. And of those commandments which are applicable today the truth is that they only take up a small percentage of the average Jew's day. There is, consequently, an enormous range of daily life which does not fall explicitly under the obligation of a "duty of the limb."

On the other hand, there is an entire field of opportunity called the "duties of the heart," which encompass a person's inner world, his attitude toward everyone, everything, and every situation he encounters. A person, for instance, can say his blessing over food before partaking of it, but does he feel gratitude in his heart that his Creator made such food? That is a duty of the heart. A person can fill by rote all the daily obligations the *Shulchan Aruch* details, but is he happy simply to be alive and have the privilege to serve His Maker? When one becomes conscious of the "duties of the heart," then *all* life becomes, potentially, one long chain of serving G–d, of fulfilling His will.

There are people who truly are happy merely to be alive — and you can see it on their faces. They radiate life. And the reason is because every second of life to them is a an accomplishment. Every moment is an opportunity to ask: How does G–d expect me to feel, think, react? I can fulfill my duty of the heart in every situation. (See Chapter 1.)

There is enormous power in truly possessing this state of mind. And because it is ultimately a state of mind it is up to us to make the choice to acquire it or not. Moreover, such a person will ultimately perform the *mitzvos* better. If his purpose is frustrated — whether that purpose be a mundane goal or even a spiritual one — his performance will not suffer.

For instance, if he spiritually falls short in some way — he even does a serious sin — he will not throw up his hands in defeat and say, "Well, there's no sense trying to be a good person. I'm already tainted with sin. I might as well continue to do it." The person who sees every moment as another opportunity to serve G–d's will will not easily succumb to that type of thinking.

Instead, he will say, "I have sinned. I have lost a great opportunity. But I can make up for it. No matter how much I failed I can always do *teshuva*; my Maker is always accessible to my prayers and sincere desire to reconnect to Him even after I fail." That is fulfilling a duty of the heart.

Everyone is prone to sin; everyone is going to fall short at least once and probably a lot more in life. The real problems begin, however, when we allow ourselves to feel

SO ON EARTH

worthless or crestfallen *after* we sin. Getting depressed compounds the mistake. After the sin we have the responsibility to seek out G–d's favor and reestablish our relationship with Him. That is *teshuva*. But when we sin and think it is not worth it to regain our previous level we enlarge the sin. That is why every sin is potentially only *part* of the sin. If we let it get us down to the point where we spiral downwards spiritually, then we have really lost touch with the purpose of our lives.

The person who has trained himself to appreciate life and value every moment will have greater resiliency to bounce back. He is never overwhelmed with feelings of worthlessness. He is used to feeling the meaning and beauty of every simple moment. If he fails he feels bad; if he has goals he feels down when they are frustrated — but since he knows that life has value each moment, then he can more easily overcome setbacks and failures.

We can view our inner life, then, in two ways: As a domain where we have few if any obligations or as one where we have self-directed obligations. The former is in essence similar to Adam's understanding of *ochal tochal*. Adam ate from the other trees, and even though his eating was a fulfillment of G–d's will he was not conscious of that fact. That made his eating nothing more than a mundane act.

If, on the other hand, he had been conscious of the necessity to fulfill the "duties of the heart," then he would have realized that the simple act of eating is a great chance to express gratitude to his Creator for the opportunity to fulfill

His will in this world. If Adam had been conscious that enjoying life could be a duty of the heart, then he would have been enveloped in an aura of holiness which would have protected him from the wiles of the primordial snake. He wasn't. And that opened the door to sin.

We do not want to open the door to sin. Today, even with the door shut it lurks all about and threatens to seep inside. The only solution is to become an inwardly fortified person. Such a person can conceivably walk through Times Square and be insulated from evil. On the other hand, a person whose limbs are performing commandments but whose mind is blank — or worse, whose mind is in the street — is prone to seduction to the primordial snake. Becoming a "duties-of-the-heart" Jew is therefore perhaps more important today than ever before. It is the best insurance one can acquire to avoid the trouble Adam opened himself up to.

CHAPTER 14

Garments Of Light, Garments Of Skin

- *Explaining the "garments of skin" G–d garbed Adam in, the relationship between clothing and embarrassment, how to turn "skin" into "light," the history of Adam's garment, the secret of every hunter, and the dual nature of our garment: the body.*

And *Hashem*/G–d made for the man and his wife garments of skin, and clothed them. (Genesis 3:21)

The Biblical word for "skin" is *or*, which begins with the Hebrew letter *ayin*. The Sages, though, explain that the word can be read as if it began with an *alef*, which would change the meaning of the word from "skin" to "light."[84] (An *ayin* and *alef* are almost identical letters.[85]) In other words, according to the second reading, G–d dressed Adam and Chava in "garments of light." What does it mean? What is the difference?

AS IN HEAVEN

Clothing and Embarrassment

Before their sin Adam and Chava were naked, *yet **not** embarrassed*. The reason was because in their original creation their bodies were just as spiritually pure and beautiful as their souls. As in heaven so on earth. Earth in its original form mirrored the perfection of heaven. (See Introduction.) Anything that G–d created in its original form is holy through and through. It has nothing to hide.

Adam and Chava, however, sinned. A sin is by definition use of the human body in a way that is against G–d's will. And that is what was embarrassing for them. They had gone against G–d's will and knew it.

Picture a common thief. He steals something from a store and hides it in his pocket. Suddenly, the security guard comes over to him and, as people say, he gets caught "red-handed." He gets exposed. If he never had anything in his pocket to begin with he would never have had anything to be embarrassed about.

Adam and Chava "stole" something. They ate the fruit they were told not to eat. When G–d "caught" them they were embarrassed. They were no less naked than before the sin. Now, however, they had something to hide. And that was their embarrassment. Beforehand they did not mind being transparent. After they committed their sin, however, they had something to hide and consequently their nakedness — their inability to cover up — became an embarrassment to them.

SO ON EARTH

Busha, Levush, Teshuva

G–d, however, enclothed them. The word "to enclothe," *levush* (from *vayalbeeshaim*, "And He enclothed them") shares the same root as the word *busha*, meaning "embarrassment." The connection is obvious. Wherever one feels embarrassment the urge is to cover the embarrassment, to "cover up" and dress up in "clothes."

This is why it is said that "clothes make the person." You can tell a great deal about a person by the clothes he wears. The clothing (*levush*) is an expression of the inner embarrassment (*busha*). If, for instance, you are embarrassed that you are Jewish you dress like a non-Jew. The clothes reveal the insides of the wearer.

Adam and Chava could no longer be proud of their status. G–d created them with pure, holy bodies. They stained them, though, and could not hide the fact. So, G–d gave them "garments of skin." Skin is literally a cover for the inner organs. The "garments of *skin*" G–d enclothed them with, therefore, signified that they had an embarrassment they needed to cover up.

In the alternate reading, however, G–d gave them "garments of light." This was an expression of their *potential*. When a person stained with sin purifies himself his outer appearance once again becomes a clear glass container through which his inner light radiates with its full intensity. This is called transforming one's "garments of skin" into "garments of light." (Transforming the *ayin* into an *alef*.)

This is the point: If we have an inner embarrassment we will find ourselves trying to cover up. Sins can be made up for and expiated, though. This is the idea of *teshuva* (which is spelled similarly to *busha*, embarrassment). *Teshuva* "transforms" our *busha* into a *levush or*; it "returns" our embarrassing garments-of-skin back into garments-of-light. Our outsides, now purified, once more become clear vessels through which our original inner beauty radiates outwards. In the broad sense, *teshuva* makes earth (the body) a perfect reflection of heaven (the soul). That is the goal.

The History of the Garments

Our Sages teach that Adam's garment was passed down through the generations. Noah had it in the ark. He gave it to his sons.[86] It was eventually misappropriated by the evil monarch Nimrod,[87] who used it in his campaign to convince everyone that he was a god. Esau eventually procured it from Nimrod,[88] where it became a permanent possession of Yitzchak's (Isaac's) family. When Yaakov (Jacob) went to get the blessings from his father and dressed up in garments to fool him into thinking he was Esau, it was this garment which he wore.[89] That is why when Yaakov entered dressed in the garment Yitzchak comments, "The smell of my son is like the smell of a *field* G–d has blessed [i.e. the Garden of Eden[90]]."[91] It was literally the Garden of Eden from whence this garment originated.

SO ON EARTH

The Hunter's Garment

Esau, on the other hand, was known as a hunter,[92] and, in fact, he would use the garment in his hunting ventures. When you think about it this makes a lot of sense. Consider the skill of hunter. A hunter has to trap an unsuspecting animal. If the animal sees the hunter it will run away. The real reason that an animal runs from a person — the root of its fear — is the Divine Image, the *tzelem Elokim*, in which the human being was created.[93] For a hunter, though, the animal's fear of him is not good. If they fear they will run away. Therefore, the human hunter must somehow camouflage himself.

This is what Esau did. He grew up in the house of Yitzchak, the holy man par excellence. In order to succeed as a hunter he had to figure out a way to cover up his inherent holiness. Therefore, Esau camouflaged his *tzelem Elokim*. He became a low, materialistic person. He used the garment as a "garment of skin." This allowed him to trap animals.

You Wear What You Are

We learn an extremely important lesson from this. Even though the garment has special qualities, nevertheless whether it will serve as a "garment of skin" or a "garment of light" *is determined solely by the free will of the wearer.*[94] If a righteous person such as Yaakov wears it it becomes a garment wherein one recognizes the fragrance of the Garden of Eden. If that same garment is used by an evil person, such as Esau, the archetypal hunter, then indeed it is a "garment of skin." This proves that it is not the garment which is the main thing, but the free will of a human being.

A Robe of Majesty

Looking at the idea of "garments of light" and "garments of skin" on a universal level we see a very relevant lesson. Each human being is a spiritual entity given the garb of a physical body. The body is an incredible tool with unbelievable qualities. However, it is like Adam's garment. It can go either way. If it allows the soul to shine in all its splendor, then an inner light radiates from within. The body can be said to be a "garment of light," which enables the beauty of our deepest selves to be transparent to all.

If, on the other hand, we become immersed in materialistic longings — lust, greed, jealousy — to the point where we are stained with actions that cause our soul embarrassment, then our bodies will become nothing more than "garments of skin." Our divine image will not shine through.

We are not great by virtue of the body; it is not what bestows grandeur upon us. The soul is the true source of human majesty. Our goal is use our free will to choose to be a Yaakov, not an Esau — and thereby make our insides shine through so that even the body becomes a robe of majesty. When we do, then all who look upon us will say "there is no iniquity in Yaakov."[95] They will acknowledge that we wear "garments of light."

CHAPTER 15

Cain And Abel

- *Explaining the incident between Cain and Abel, the meaning of their names, ego-centricity versus humility, Capitalism versus Socialism, and Abraham's synthesis.*

Every detail enumerated in these early chapters is monumental. The Torah includes the stories of early civilization[96] because they contain the root causes of all we experience today — the good and the bad. Indeed, the very psychology of murder itself is hinted to in the very names of the first murderer and murder victim.

Cain

Cain's name not only described his mother's reasons for naming him but his central character trait.

> And Adam knew his wife Chava, and she conceived and bore Cain, saying, "I have acquired a man with[97] *Hashem.*" (Genesis 4:1)

Canisi ("I have acquired") is similar to "Cain." Cain's main character trait was the acquisitive instinct, which can be good because an acquisition is something a person attains through effort; it is not a gift. The positive purpose of Cain's acquisitive instinct was to use it in becoming a partner with G–d in creation. G–d wants human beings to put forth effort in acquiring their share in bringing about the perfection of creation. This was the higher objective of bestowing Cain with an acquisitive instinct. He was endowed with the ability to take the initiative, to seek to acquire — in other words, he was given a certain amount of ego, which is good and necessary in proper dosages. The fact that he misused it does not make the trait inherently bad.

Hevel

By contrast, Abel, which in Hebrew is pronounced *hevel*, means "air." Whereas Cain represents the instinct to acquire — which in a positive sense is the instinct of self, as in the famous aphorism of Hillel, "If I am not for myself, who will be?"[98] — Abel represents the opposite: air, nothingness, emptiness, or the second part of Hillel's aphorism, "Yet, if I am only for myself, what am I?"

Cain was born first because a sense of self is the foremost quality a human being needs in order to succeed in the world. Without self a human being can be no more than a recipient — not an initiator or a creator. Abel's name teaches us, however, that one's sense of self must not lead to ego-centricity, but has to be tempered with humility.

SO ON EARTH

Set-up for Murder

We can see how these personality distinctions led directly to the murder.

> Abel became a shepherd and Cain became a tiller of the ground. After some time, Cain brought an offering to G–d from the fruit of the ground. And Abel also brought from the first-born and best-parts of his flock. G–d was pleased with Abel and his offering, whereas concerning Cain and his offering He was not pleased. Cain got very angry and his face fell. (Genesis 4:2-5)

When you are ego-centric you are reluctant to give up any of your possessions — and if you do give them up you are loathe to give your best. That was Cain. Cain's offering was not pleasing because he did not bring from the best of his produce; he brought second class goods. His ego-centricity did not allow him to give with a full heart.

On the other hand, when you are overly self-effacing you lack initiative. That is why it says that Abel "also" brought his offering: *he did not bring it until he first saw that his brother brought one.* Once he brought it, though, he did not mind bringing the best of his possessions because his ego was not driving him to be selfish in any way.

Every successful human being has to be some combination of these Cain and Abel qualities. On one hand, a person has to have enough self-image to realize the necessity of taking matters into his own hands, of taking

AS IN HEAVEN

responsibility. On the other hand, a person has to possess true humility.

The tragedy of Cain and Abel comes about because each was incomplete alone and unable to learn from the other. Cain was excessively self-oriented to the point of egocentricity while Abel was excessively self-effacing to the point of ineffectualness. The inability to learn from each other led to their downfall. Alone, they were incomplete and setting themselves up for disaster.

The Psychology of Blame

Cain was upset when his offering was not accepted like his brother's because he thought, "Isn't it enough that I brought You, G–d, an offering? Isn't it enough that I acknowledge You?" He thought he was so great that it was enough for him to merely recognize his duty to G–d. His ego did not let him see that he was not performing any favors for G–d by doing a half-baked job.

And this leads us into a very interesting and important psychological insight. When Cain sees that G–d is not pleased with his actions, he ideally should have concluded, "I have to improve myself." Instead, what does he do? He looks for excuses. He looks to pin the blame on others.

This is humanity's downfall. It is one thing to make a mistake, to fall short. It is another thing, though, to compound the mistake by failing to correct it. What prevented Cain from taking corrective actions? His ego.

SO ON EARTH

"Me? Cain, the son of Adam? I should be treated like this? There can't be any fault in me. If my brother didn't try to show off by bringing the best of his flock I wouldn't have had any problems. Abel — he's the one who is making my life miserable."

Consequently, he murdered Abel. He thought he was eliminating the source of his problems. In reality, though, he was only compounding them. Failure to improve ourselves at the core is its own sin and leads to a self-perpetuating cycle of failure, blame, and evil.

The failure of Cain and Abel is a human tragedy, one subsequent humanity has still yet to learn from. The world is still plagued with egotistical murderers and self-denying victims. However, perhaps even more tragic than all the individual Cain-and-Abel murders and encounters that have plagued humanity throughout history is the embodiment of Cain-Abel personalities in a much larger arena: in two of the greatest ideological movements civilization has known.

The Two Ideologies

Adam was created alone. He opened his eyes and saw an entire world before him. Cain was Adam's firstborn. He opened his eyes and saw that the entire world belonged to his father. Naturally, he thought he was going to inherit it *all* from his father one day.

Then, suddenly, Abel came into the picture.

"Who are you?" Cain asked.

AS IN HEAVEN

"I'm your brother. We have to share the world between us."

"No way. My father received the entire world and I will get the entire world from him. There is nothing to share. In fact, you belong to me. If you try to take any part of the world from me I will kill you."

Cain was the first Capitalist.

Half the world was not enough. He did not want to share one blade of grass in it with anyone else, even his brother. It was not sufficient to have more than he needed, more than he could ever use. He wanted everything he could get his hands on. And he could not stand the thought of another human being possessing something he believed was his — and he believed everything was his! Cain was a hard core Capitalist in the classic sense, driven to acquire and possess everything he could get his hands on.

Abel, on the other hand, came to his brother with the argument that the world was big enough to share between them. Born second, he had no pretensions he was going to possess everything. His reasoning sounds altruistic, but in reality it was not necessarily so. *It was his secondary position and lack of initiative which led him* to develop the philosophy that everything had to be shared equally, not necessarily his idealistic nature.

He was the first Communist.

The conflict between Capitalist and Communist (which we will explain in more detail just ahead) did not end with the death of Abel. Afterward, the philosophy of Cain

SO ON EARTH

flourished and became the dominant philosophy for the next ten generations until the time of the Flood. "The entire world belongs to me," and, "Looking out for number one," could be heard in the town halls and read in the local tabloids. The ugly side of the acquisitive instinct, the drive for personal power to the exclusion of others, dominated all humanity. No one had any respect for the possessions of anyone else. They all thought they had a right to whatever they could get their hands on. It was a world plagued with theft, robbery, adultery, etc.

After the Flood people had to give the matter second thought. Capitalism was clearly wrong. Otherwise, G–d would not have destroyed civilization as He had. Abel must have been right. G–d must desire selfless Communism therefore.

Consequently, for the next ten generations the world practiced a form of Communism. The apex of this early form of Communist politics occurred with the building of the Tower of Babel when all humanity became united under one banner. The Tower became what in modern times is called the State. It was the Center toward which all individuals invested their efforts and even gave up their individuality in order to perpetuate its existence. (See Chapter 18.)

Of course, we can assume that the Communist ideal back then was promoted to sound just as nice as it was promoted in this century. The Communist can always be found espousing his philosophy, his ideology. He continually

AS IN HEAVEN

emphasizes noble ideals like human equality, camaraderie, elimination of poverty, the ultimate good for the people, and so on *ad nauseam*. And yet in the end more people — tens and tens of millions just this century — have been killed in the name of Socialism-Communism. Why?

Because *they worship a false god: the State.*

And isn't it interesting that Communism almost invariably occurs side-by side with atheism? The reason, in my opinion, is because the human being must worship something bigger than himself, and if that something is not G–d then he has to worship — invest his ego-energies into — something like the State or the Tower. The downfall of the Communist State comes about because inevitably *the Communist man is made in the State's image, not G–d's* and the State is a collective which cannot ultimately tolerate the individual. G–d's image, on the other hand, simultaneously includes the individual and the collective, the one and the many.

Interestingly, while Communism and atheism are usually found side-by-side, in Capitalist countries this is not so: Capitalism does not go hand in hand with outright atheism. The reason is because to the capitalist *money replaces G–d*. After all, on every dollar bill (and only on the dollar) it says, "In G–d we trust." *The dollar bill is G–d!* There is no other ideology necessary therefore. Money creates its own morality. Deception is tolerable (if not advocated) if it can be shown to benefit the bottom line, if it can be rationalized to strengthen the business. Belief in the real G–d exists in the heart of the Capitalist, but no further. He only gives belief in G–d lip service. His real G–d is the all-mighty, holy Dollar (capital "D").

Communism, Abel's philosophy, had conquered in the time of the Tower of Babel. The world was united. The problem was that they were united for the wrong cause: to fight G–d; to go up to heaven, so to speak, dethrone G–d, and make a name for themselves in His place. (See Chapter 18.) G–d's response was to break up their unity by separating them into different languages. (And we have witnessed the same in our day. When the Soviet Union broke up, suddenly the myriad ethnic groups within it vied for their independence. No one could get along with anyone else. This is what happened to the generation which built the Tower of Babel.)

Abraham, who was born around that time, was caught in the middle. Cain's philosophy had been proven wrong. And then Abel's philosophy had been proven wrong. Which was the right way? Abraham eventually realized that it was a combination of both which was right.

G–d created the world with a single man and therefore as the Talmud says, "Everyone is obligated to say that for me the entire world was created."[99] On the other hand, we live in a world of others and therefore humility is an absolute necessity. We cannot be so selfish that we trample over others in the process. We cannot lose our ethics because of fear of another's success. We must share the wealth, the fame, the glory and realize doing so in no way diminishes from our own. We must give credit where credit is due and not lead others to believe the credit was ours when in fact it was not.

Self and humility. These are the hallmarks of the whole person, of the whole society. Anything less is a fragmentation that will ultimately lead to no good. Hopefully, one day we will all learn from the tragic failure of Cain and Abel and seek to become more like Abraham who was able to synthesize the two into one.

CHAPTER 16

The Eve Of Disaster

- *Explaining Noah's life and times before the Flood, the power of the individual, the crucial difference between Noah and Abraham, the secret to becoming a master teacher, why theft triggers punishment and destruction, building an ark today, and the secret to lasting success.*

And *Hashem* saw how great was the evil of man on the earth, for the entire inclination of the thoughts of his heart were only evil all day . . . But Noah found favor in the eyes of *Hashem*. (Genesis 6:5,8)

How great is the power of the individual! The entire world can turn corrupt, but all it takes is one individual to go against the tide to be its salvation. We, too, have to see ourselves as individuals. If the world around us is flooded with evil — if those in our vicinity are driven by raw greed and debased desires — there is still no reason to despair.

AS IN HEAVEN

You could still be a Noah. You could still be a person worthy of salvation through whom the rest of the world eventually gets rebuilt.

Noah's True Offspring

> These are the generations of Noah: Noah was a man righteous [and] perfect in his generation. Noah walked with G‑d. Noah bore three sons: Shem, Cham, and Yefes. (Genesis 6:9-10)

This sequence of information is problematic. After the verse says: "These are the generations of Noah. . ." we would expect it to say: "Shem, Cham, and Yefes." However, instead it says: "These are the generations of Noah: *Noah. . .*" as if to say that Noah was his own offspring! And indeed he was, for the true offspring ("generations," "progeny") of a righteous person are his good deeds.[100]

The Brisker Rav once asked a wealthy man, "How come you are not involved in learning Torah or giving to charitable causes? All you do is work and work and work all day, day after day."

"Rabbi," the man answered, "I'm doing it for my children."

The Rav answered, "Don't you know that your father also did the same thing for his children? And his father for his children. Everyone was doing it for his children. Where, I ask, is the child everyone is working so hard for? Show me the child."

SO ON EARTH

We have to remember that while we are busy all day working for our children, we too are someone's child. "These are the children of Noah: Noah..." A righteous man's true offspring are his good deeds. If you first make yourself worthy and righteous (at least to the best of your ability), your children will have a better chance to become worthy and righteous. If you neglect yourself, then your children are probably going to learn to neglect themselves — and so on... until hopefully one child finally figures out what is going on and takes it upon his shoulders to make himself truly worthy and righteous. Why not be that child yourself?

The Difference Between Noah and Abraham

Noah was a man righteous [and] perfect in his generation. (Genesis 6:9)

What is added by the statement: "... in his generation." Does it give additional praise to Noah or the opposite? The Sages are divided.[101] One explains it that if Noah was righteous in his generation — which was such a debased generation — how much more righteous would he have been in another generation. The other opinion sees the statement as limiting Noah's righteousness: he was righteous only *in comparison* to his generation, i.e. *within* his generation. Had Noah been in Abraham's generation his righteousness would have counted for nothing.

The Eve Of Disaster 209

AS IN HEAVEN

According to the first opinion, had Noah lived in Abraham's generation he would have in effect become an Abraham. In the latter scenario, the Sages are telling us that there is an intrinsic distinction between Noah and Abraham. What exactly was the difference?

> Noah walked with G–d. (Genesis 8:9)

Noah is described as someone who walked *with* G–d. Abraham on the other hand is described differently:

> When Abram was ninety-nine, G–d appeared to him and said, "I am the Almighty G–d. Walk before Me and be perfect." (Genesis 17:1)

Abraham was told to walk *before* G–d. The difference between walking *with* someone versus walking *before* someone is the difference between an employee and a partner (see Chapter 5). Noah was an employee. He only went *with* G–d. He was not shown the confidence to be granted the *independence* a partner enjoys. Abraham, however, was told, "Walk before Me. . ." To walk *before* or in front of G–d, so to speak, means that the person is encouraged to display a greater degree of independence than someone who merely walks *with* G–d. Only Abraham was told to walk before Him because he was carving out a new path, a path greater than the one established previously by Noah.

Just as G–d told Abraham to walk before Him, Abraham taught people to walk before him. "Educate the child according *to his way...*"[102] Abraham was the educator par excellence and indeed had many disciples. True, they were eventually lost to history; we do not know what happened to all the people Abraham brought to belief in G–d. We do know, however, what happened to his greatest disciple: his son, Yitzchak. Yitzchak was someone whose service to G–d was of an entirely different variety than Abraham's — and yet it was still perfectly valid. There are many legitimate ways to serve G–d. Abraham's greatness as a teacher lay in the fact that he did not try to make people over in his image — he tried to bring out the individuality of each disciple and give him the ability to go down his own path.

Abraham was not interested in making a following of followers. Rather he wanted them to follow their own individual paths toward serving the one, true G–d. That is what made him the teacher par excellence. He did not impose his expectations upon those he had influence on. He observed their particular gifts and talents and helped them discover their own authentic spiritual individuality.

This is one of the characteristics of a partner: he is independent and therefore encourages independence. Noah, by contrast, did not have this degree of initiative, nor did he engender it in others. That is why he did not ultimately win over his generation. He maintained his righteousness in the face of all opposition, but he did not win over the opposition to his side. The world, consequently, was destroyed in his day. Noah was a good employee. He did his job. But he was not enough to save the "business."

AS IN HEAVEN

The Sin that Sunk the Generation

And G–d said to Noah: "The end of all flesh has come before Me, for the earth is filled with robbery through them. And behold I will destroy them with the earth." (Genesis 6:13)

The Torah teaches that although Noah's generation was guilty of many transgressions — adultery, idol worship, and much more — the edict of destruction was not decreed against them until they sunk to *chamas*, which means "robbery."[103] From this we see that although a person can be guilty of many transgressions he is not necessarily punished for them immediately. Thievery, however, can trigger it all. When one is finally reduced to robbery he opens himself up to the possibility that all his transgressions will be paid up.

Why is robbery worse than other sins? The answer is that acknowledging the boundaries which separate one person's property from another's is a primary foundation upon which society stands. That is why one-fourth of the entire code of Jewish law, the *Shulchan Aruch,* is devoted exclusively to monetary laws. The most reliable measuring rod of a Jew's commitment to the ideals of Torah is that he is honest and straight-forward in his monetary dealings.

It goes beyond this, however. Acknowledging the boundaries of ownership is not only the testing ground for one's commitment to absolute truth and justice. *It is a prerequisite for existing in the world.* Each person is given by G–d (via divine providence[104]) his personal property and private domain through which he is expected to complete

SO ON EARTH

his mission in the world. If another person steals his property he has lost a vehicle allotted him by G–d to complete his purpose. The one who steals, therefore, not only violates the property of another, but demonstrates that he has violated the basic respect for another person's mission in life.

Indeed, when people lose sight of or actively transgress the oftentimes fine line that separates an honest business practice from a dishonest one it is not only a sin, but the very fabric of society — of the ability of human beings to relate to each other in a decent way — is torn apart. And it does not matter how spiritual or scholarly one is otherwise. Stealing is not a matter of religion, per say. It is a matter of violating the basic ability of human beings to have a relationship with each other. When all respect for other human beings and their property ceases to exist the members of that society forfeit their right of existence. When everyone is stealing from everyone else no one can fulfill his purpose. That is why the transgression which triggered the flood was robbery.

Make an Ark

G–d's response to the degenerate behavior of the generation was to tell Noah to build an ark. The ark symbolizes shelter. The message for us is that even amidst a world sunk in the lowest behaviors a person can nevertheless carve out a shelter for himself where the outside influences do not enter. He can avoid physical destruction and, just as

AS IN HEAVEN

importantly, the destruction to his character, by building an "ark" where the flood-waters of strife and dishonesty inundating the world do not affect him.

The word "ark" (*teyva*) has another meaning in Hebrew: "word." When the world about is going insane a Jew can lock himself and his family inside the "word" of Torah. Torah — not just book knowledge, but actually living the Torah — is a protection from the negative influences of society raging about.

Let me offer one practical example. Imagine owning a piece of real estate that has a particular drawback to it. An anxious potential buyer approaches you and would buy it without much investigation into the problems with the property. You are in a dilemma: If you tell him about the drawback he might turn down the deal. If, on the other hand, you come up with the rationale that by withholding the information you may not be technically at fault (because, after all, the buyer should have done his homework) you may make some money. Nevertheless, the truly straight-forward thing would be to inform him of the drawback and trust that G–d will make your endeavors no less profitable in the end.

There is potentially a lot of money which can be made dishonestly nowadays. If one makes money but eventually loses it — especially if the loss comes about through peculiar circumstances — that may well be a sign that the money was not legitimately earned to begin with. *Honest money does not go lost.* Dishonest money is volatile. As the

SO ON EARTH

saying goes: "Dishonesty has no feet,"[105] which means that it will not last for long. "Truth," on the other hand, "stands forever."[106]

"Truth sprouts from the earth."[107] Truth is like a seed. At first the seed must be put in the ground and allowed to decay. So, too, honesty at first appears to have disadvantages. Your potential profits decay and rot away. People tell you you will never make a living conducting business so honestly. However, like a seed, eventually your honesty will begin to sprout. That is what "Truth sprouts from the earth" means. Truth is a long-term investment. The investor needs patience and trust. In the end, though, he will see fruits — legitimately-earned fruits.

Therefore, no matter what situation you are in there is no justification for the excuse: "Well, everyone else does it." One has to always remember that no matter how much the flood-waters rage about for the time being they will eventually pass. Therefore, if you cannot save the world, at least shelter yourself and your family inside an "ark."

A Jew's ark is the "word" of Torah. The least a person can do is build himself an ark — a bastion of Torah — and be patient, knowing that his honesty and commitment to Torah values is going to outdistance the dishonesty and destruction rampaging about.

CHAPTER 17

After The Flood

- *Explaining the verses describing the events just after the Flood, the hidden code of "Hitler," why we are allowed to eat meat, the three decision-making centers in each human being, the ramifications of Noah's drunkenness, what to do with yearnings for mysticism, and the difference between Kabbalah and Hasidism.*

And Noah built an altar to *Hashem*; and took of every clean beast, and of every bird, and offered burnt offerings on the altar. And *Hashem* smelled the pleasing aroma. Then *Hashem* said to Himself, "No more will I destroy the earth because of man, for the inclination of the heart of man is evil from his youth. . ." (Genesis 8:20-21)

Noah emerged from the ark into a "post-Holocaust" world. Surveying the aftermath, his emotions surged with a deep desire to express every tortured longing in his soul. So, he built an altar and offered sacrifices. The Torah then says that G–d was pleased with the aroma of these sacrifices. The obvious question is: Does the smell of roasted meat really please G–d? Since it obviously does not, what

SO ON EARTH

does the verse mean? The answer is that it was not the meat but the *intention* behind the offerings which G–d found pleasing. Exactly what intention did He "smell"? For a deeper understanding we need to turn to the words of the Sages.

> The pleasing aroma which G–d smelled was the aroma of his [Noah's] descendant Abraham who would be willing to be thrown into the fiery furnace for G–d's sake. (*Midrash*[108])

Abraham was tested ten times. One of the tests occurred when he was thrown into a furnace because he refused to renounce his belief in the one, true G–d. That willingness to sacrifice his life is the "aroma" G–d "smelled" in Noah's sacrifice. Noah's act foreshadowed the self-sacrifice which would one day sprout forth in all its fullness in the person of Abraham.

The Sages tell us further that the "pleasing aroma" contained additional intimations of future self-sacrifice. It also intimated to the self-sacrifice of Chananiah, Mishael, and Azariah — the three Jewish youths who were thrown into the fiery furnace of King Nebuchadnezzar.[109] Like Abraham, they too were completely prepared to give up their lives rather than submit to a depraved ruler's request that they bow to an idol. And, like Abraham, G–d miraculously saved them and let them walk out of the fire unscathed.

Finally, the above teaching of the Sages adds, at the moment Noah was performing his sacrifices the pleasing aroma of yet a third future act of Jewish self-sacrifice was detectable: the sacrifice of the "generation of *shmad.*" *Shmad* generally means destruction through persecution, but can just as easily be translated as "genocide" or "holocaust." In fact, one of the commentators on the *Midrash* elaborates on the sacrifice of the generation of *shmad* as follows:

> Although Abraham, as well as Chananiah, Mishael, and Azariah, were miraculously saved from the fiery furnace, the generation of *shmad* will not. This generation will give up their lives sanctifying G-d's name, and actually have their bodies burned up.[110]

This comment is especially eerie when we consider the generation of *shmad* which we were witness to not long ago, the generation which perished in the gas chambers and furnaces of the Nazi Holocaust. Yet, the author of the comment penned it long before! Even more remarkable, this comment is supported by a discovery only first made available with the advent of computer technology.

For more than a decade now computers have been programmed to search the Torah for "hidden codes."[111] The codes, embedded as single letters spaced at even intervals throughout the Hebrew text (for example, every 50th letter) form words, phrases, and sentences which demonstrate the supernatural origin of the Torah. Relevant to our topic, a computer was programmed to search the Book of Genesis to locate where the Hebrew equivalent of "Hitler" was spelled out in the smallest interval code. (The "smallest

SO ON EARTH

interval" means that even if the five letter name *heh-yud-tes-lamed-raish* [Hitler] was embedded in more than one place, the computer would identify the place where *the smallest dispersion* between these letters could be found.[112])

The computer searched and found that indeed Hitler's name was encoded in the Torah. It occurred at the smallest interval in one place at an interval of thirty-one[113] letters — and, incredibly, that place was our passage where G–d smelled "the pleasing aroma" of the generation of *shmad* which would be completely consumed in the furnace! In other words, here is a code embedded in the ancient text of the Torah which unmistakably connects "Hitler" with Jewish bodies getting burned up in a furnace as the result of *shmad*, holocaust!

Subsequent research revealed that not only was Hitler's name interwoven through this passage, but the highest concentration of lowest interval codes related to the Holocaust were there as well, for instance: the Hebrew equivalents of Berlin, Germany, Nazi, Auschwitz, gas chamber, Eichman, swastika (and others).

The real importance of this code is the message it supports: if any generation was the generation of *shmad* it was the generation which perished in the gas chambers and furnaces of the Nazi Holocaust. It ties their destiny to the acts of Abraham, Chananiah, Mishael, and Azariah in one 3,800-year-long chain. Abraham — the beginning of the Jewish nation — was willing to give up his life in order not to desecrate the name of G–d in the eyes of others. This

After The Flood 219

essential trait in Abraham manifested itself generations later in Chananiah, Mishael, and Azariah.[114] In our century, the generation of *shmad* — the generation of the Holocaust — links together all the sacrifices of prior Jewish history. They represent the ultimate testing ground — the graduating experience, if you will — of the Jewish People. It is they more so than any previous generation who testify to Abraham's essential character: identification with the values of eternity even to the point of death.[115]

If so, then, the generation of the Holocaust literally was the generation of *shmad* which G–d "smelled" at the time of Noah. He "smelled" their capacity for sacrifice. He saw in Noah a seed — in the form of Abraham and his descendants — from which He could rebuild the entire world. And that explains why the aroma was so "pleasing" to G–d. Despite the fact that imperfection, and even the potential for evil, still existed in Noah, the genuine feeling behind his offering led G–d to declare: "No more will I destroy the earth because of man. . ." Through Abraham — the future embodiment of total self-sacrifice latent in Noah — the world had a vessel to bring ultimate redemption.

Permission to Eat Meat

> And G–d blessed Noah and his sons saying, "Be fruitful and multiply and fill the earth. And the fear of you and the dread of you shall be upon every animal of the earth and all the birds of the sky, and in all that crawls on the ground, as well as in all the fish in the sea — in your hand they are given. Every moving thing that lives shall be food for you;

SO ON EARTH

as the green herbage I give you everything. . ." (Genesis 9:1-3)

On an airline once, I had an interesting conversation with a passenger. It began when the flight attendant came by to hand us our meals. The man next to me took his prepackaged meal and watched with interest as I turned down the airline's meal and instead took out a prepared salad from my briefcase. Curiosity brimming, the passenger turned to me and asked, "What's the matter, you don't eat meat?"

"What makes you think so?" I responded.

"Because I see you didn't take the airline's meal."

"No, I eat meat," I assured him. "But we Jews have a special diet. I eat meat only if it is *kosher* and prepared in a *kosher* way." As he thought about my response, I couldn't resist the urge so I asked: "Do you mind if I ask you a question? Why do you eat meat?"

"Me?" he responded as he dug into his steak. "Why not?"

"Tell me," I said, "did you ever hear of the Old Testament?"

"Of course."

"Do you believe G–d created the world?"

He chuckled and then said, "No."

"How, then, do you believe the world came to be?" I asked.

"Haven't you heard of Darwin?"

He thought that was the end of the conversation, but then I added, "If you believe in Darwin then let me ask you this: by what right do you eat this meat?"

"Why not?" he asked surprised.

"Don't you know, it may be a distant cousin or long lost relative . . . . Just because this steak is a little less evolved than you, what right do you have to eat it? Give it a little more time and one day an ancestor of yours may marry its ancestor. What's the difference between it and a human being?"

He was speechless. Then, he laughed and said, "You know, you have a point." I thought the conversation was ended, but then he asked me a question: "Tell me, though, by what right do *you* eat meat?"

"Since," I responded, "I believe that G–d created the world, I open up the Bible and find out what man's right is. And our Bible tells us that the Creator gave the human race everything in the world to use — as long as it is used in the prescribed way. Therefore, I know what I can eat and how I am allowed to go about eating it."

Taking animal life is not a simple matter. G–d therefore gave the Jewish People very precise, restrictive laws what to eat and how to prepare it. One of the effects of these restrictions is to increase our sensitivity to both the act of slaughtering and the act of eating. Originally, though, G–d did not allow human beings to take animal life for consumption needs.[116] That permission first came only after Noah left of the ark. And, still, even then the permission was with a restriction. (They were not required to keep the complex dietary laws given later at Sinai, but they were forbidden to eat the "limb of a live animal."[117]) However,

SO ON EARTH

beyond the sensitizing process that slaughtering with restrictions induces there was a deeper reason why eating meat was permitted at that time.

Human nature had undergone a monumental change in the generations leading up to the Flood. Originally, Adam's animal nature was more or less in check. As civilization unfolded, however, it began to rage out of control, so much so in fact that the animals themselves also became participants in the corrupt and perverse behavior which took place during the Generation of the Flood.[118] In actuality, however, their behavior was only the outward manifestation of human behavior. It was the animal nature within humanity which was truly corrupt and polluted.

As a consequence, permission was granted to eat meat. Eating meat in the prescribed manner is a form of *tikun*, "repair." When an animal is consumed by a person in the proper way the energy it gives the body "repairs" the damage caused earlier. *Eating, therefore, is not merely a source of energy for the body but a potential vehicle of repair.* When it is done in line with the Divine Will in an atmosphere of respect and dignity the food itself becomes elevated.

This, by the way, helps explain one reason why people should not seek to totally negate the physical — as is often the emphasis in many Eastern religions, for example. The Torah is at odds with those religions and doctrines which preach asceticism in its various forms, including celibacy, body denial, meditating all day, lying on a bed of nails, etc.

AS IN HEAVEN

Rather, the Torah says, "be fruitful and multiply," which generally means that a person must marry, raise a family, live in a home, and have an income. We are fathers, mothers, bread-winners, and builders. Even our Sabbath, the holiest day of all, is very physical. For instance, it is sanctified Friday night on a cup of wine — strong, intoxicating wine is the ideal. Then we eat, sing, and interact with our family until the following nightfall. It's all very physical.

This is not so in many non-Torah approaches, which tend to associate holiness with a person who meditates all day, fasts as much as he can, avoids all intimate relationships, denies and defies all bodily pleasures, etc. The way they conceive it, the ultimate goal is achieved when a person denies the physical plane, totally dissociating himself from and rejecting his body. In the Torah outlook this is not so. We are to partake in the physical, in the prescribed fashion, for the purposes of elevating it.

Through the commandments, which tell us how to conduct ourselves in the physical world, we sanctify the earthly and thereby transform it into a mirror of the heavenly. In the Torah outlook we are here to transform and harness every possible element of the world, not suppress or deny it. We are to partake in the physical for the purposes of elevating it.

This — and we have only touched the surface here — is one of the deeper reasons G–d gave humanity permission to eat meat. The animal nature in human beings (and the animals themselves) before the Flood had gone out of control.

SO ON EARTH

Eating meat is a way of "repairing" animal nature. When we keep this in mind and prepare our food in the way the Divine Will prescribes we are partaking in an activity that produces much more than mere palatal enjoyment and bodily nutrition. We are elevating the animal world — and, in a deeper sense, the animal nature within ourselves.

This "repair" first became necessary after the Flood. Consequently, that is when Noah and his sons were given permission to eat meat. Such permission was an early vehicle toward the goal of "repairing" animal nature polluted by the Generation of the Flood.

Shem, Cham, Yefes

The need to control our animal nature and passions is also alluded to in an entirely different set of verses which describe the situation of the world just after the Flood.

> And the sons of Noah who went out of the ark were Shem, Cham, and Yefes. Cham is the father of Canaan. These three are the sons of Noah and through them the entire earth was populated. (Genesis 9:18-19)

We as individuals make decisions and set up the social systems which govern our lives based on three principle character traits, traits that can be explained via the names of Noah's sons. Each son, in other words, embodied a specific characteristic that exists in *each* human being today.

Cham, which means "hot," represents the base, animal instincts. Impulsiveness. "Cham is the father of Canaan,"

AS IN HEAVEN

who was cursed to bear a society of slaves (Genesis 9:25). Cham is ultimately a slave to his impulsive, animal instincts; they rule him. His blood is "hot." He does whatever comes to mind without forethought or consideration. He has no conscience, no inhibitions, no personal "brakes" to stop the momentum of his animal instincts.

After all is said and done, though, everyone has a little Cham inside himself. This is the way G–d designed us. We all have been created with bodies that have instinctual needs. Satisfying the Cham instinct is necessary to a degree and important for the overall well-being of the whole person — *but it must be not be allowed to go unchecked.* It is good only when "enslaved" or harnessed in the proper way.

The second character trait bequeathed civilization from Noah's sons is the Yefes instinct. Yefes means "beauty," not in the internal sense but in the external sense. He is sensitive, like the artist, to external stimuli but he goes no deeper. Yefes is "image" — the image we want others to think about us. When a person is worried "what others will say" — that is the Yefes quality. He is entirely driven to conform with external, societal protocol.[119]

And, again, each of us has a tiny Yefes inside. A decision emanating from the Yefes quality (unlike one emanating from the Cham quality) will be filtered through the mind. However, the main consideration is what people will say. Yefes is a follower. If society is corrupt the person operating from his Yefes center will not be able to rise above the corruption: he will do whatever everyone else is doing.

SO ON EARTH

And, conversely, if he is a coarse person operating in a pious society he will put on the clothes and mask of that society, but not truly embody piety. In either scenario, the Yefes person lets others dictate his behavior. He is therefore not in touch with himself. He is a stranger to his true spiritual self.

Shem, the name of Noah's third son, means "name." We call G–d: *Hashem*, "The Name." The Shem quality is our inner voice emanating from divinity. It is our acknowledgment of the voice of Torah which emanates from Sinai. A Shem person says, "I don't care what people want. I don't even care what I think I want — I only want to do what G–d wants." Each of us has a bit of Shem inside as well.

Whenever a decision has to be made we need to ask ourselves from which center we are operating. Are we centered in Cham, impulsiveness, or Yefes, the need to conform to society, or Shem, the desire to heed the voice of truth? Our goal, of course, should be to listen to the voice of the Shem instinct. Its call is the call of Torah.

Noah Debased Himself

Noah and his sons were charged with the responsibility to rebuild civilization. Noah in particular had the opportunity to lead the way and make sure that the new world he was rebuilding would be a harmonious world in line with heavenly values. He was not to deny the earthly, as we explained above, but to work with it to make it a picture image of heaven. The Torah tells us, though, that he did not make earth into a mirror of heaven, but instead became sunk in the earthly himself.

> And Noah, a man of the ground, debased himself [*vayochel* — see Rashi] and planted a vineyard. Then he drank from the wine and became drunk. And he uncovered himself within his tent. (Genesis 9:20-21)

As Rashi translates it, Noah "debased" himself. He did something "mundane" (*vayochel*, as in *chullin*), something beneath human dignity. What did he do? He "planted a vineyard." This was a mistake with universal repercussions, for when Noah came out of the ark the entire world was before him to rebuild in whatever way he saw fit. In essence, whatever he would set out to undertake first would be an endeavor endowed with "endless blessing."

> There was once a great Rabbi whose blessings were known to always come true. A poor man with a large family came from far away to visit the Rabbi and pour out his heart over his many concerns. The Rabbi blessed him: "Go home, and I bless you that the first activity you engage in will be injected with endless bounty. Just make sure you use my blessing wisely."
> The man left the Rabbi very happy and anxious. He couldn't wait to get home. He and his wife kept a small jar of coins and therefore he decided that the first thing he would do when he got home was fiddle with the coins and thereby bring upon himself the blessing of endless wealth.
> He arrived at home in the middle of the night and hurriedly ran inside to wake up his wife. "Fast! Fast! Wake up. Give me the money. Give me the jar," he bellowed at her.

SO ON EARTH

She had been in a deep sleep and all of a sudden heard a voice demanding she give over her last few coins. The room was dark, so her first thought was that it was a robber threatening her. "I'm not giving you anything," she declared.

"Fast! Fast!" the husband demanded. "Just give me the money. Don't ask questions."

"No!"

The conversation went back and forth like this until it turned into a full-fledged argument.

And that was their "endless blessing": from that day on they fought with each other for the rest of their lives. (Dubno Maggid)

When Noah first came out of the Ark he took a look at the devastation. Not a living thing was left. The world was his to rebuild as he saw fit, for G–d had blessed him that whatever he would set out to do he would do it with "endless blessing." Rather than viewing the devastation as an opportunity to rebuild, though, the first thing he did was plant a vineyard and become drunk. He let his emotions — like regret, sadness, pity, and loneliness — overwhelm him. He did something mundane (he "debased" himself) and thereby wasted his opportunity for endless blessing on mundane concerns, something the world is still suffering from until this day.

Noah's debasement can be understood in another context as well. Debasement can result from low behavior or from holy, idealistic behavior not "based" on firm ground. That is the import of planting a vineyard before anything else. Wine is desirable, but not a staple. It is essentially a luxury. Had he planted something like wheat there would be no

AS IN HEAVEN

hunger today; the world would have had an endless amount of bread. Instead, Noah debased himself. He lost his "base." He pursued luxury before necessity. He tried building "castles in the air" rather than laying a solid foundation for the future.

Another way to relate this to our contemporary circumstances is to compare it to the situation in the Jewish world after the Holocaust. There was an opportunity to rebuild the Jewish world like never before. And, indeed, just three years after it was over there was a Jewish State. However, it was not a Torah state; rather it was a state based on secular values, led by people who actively tried to disassociate themselves from the previous 3,000 years of Torah ideals. In essence, it was a State without a base, a castle in the air.

Another "castle in the air," more and more common in today's world, is "spirituality." Of course, a person's spiritual yearnings — even a "non-religious" person's spiritual yearnings — for things like mysticism are legitimate. There is no question about that. However, Kabbalah, or mysticism, is a live wire. Learning it without first being grounded in Torah living — as well as possessing a certain level of development in spiritual character — is like letting a child into a drug store filled with harmful and even life-threatening drugs. It is an irresponsible act that can lead to more harm than good.

The Sages teach us that a child is taught the entire Torah in the womb.[120] This means that the little fetus is the greatest mystic we can imagine. The minute before he is born,

SO ON EARTH

though, an angel touches him on the lip and he forgets it all. Why does he have to forget it all? The answer is *so that he can earn it all back.* He must discover it all for himself. The fetus may be a mystic, but he is not a holy man yet. Holiness must be earned.

If a person acquires mystical knowledge and abilities before the hard work of refining his moral, spiritual, and intellectual character it is like going back to the womb — having the knowledge without having earned it. It is not you. G–d can give the mystical sensations to an animal, too, if He wanted. He gave them to you, at least potentially, though, to *earn*, not just to *have*. The mystical experience has to be earned. Without earning it you are building a castle in the air, you are Noah planting a vineyard before anything else.

What should a person do who has strong feelings for the mystical? Does he have to repress them for many years before the time he may become worthy of delving into his heart's desire? Hasidism came in part to remedy that problem. Hasidism is not Kabbalah. In the ideal sense, it is Kabbalah translated into ideas and practices which can be used in practical, day-to-day living. Hasidism gives you the taste of mysticism but in a more everyday style. In fact, those forms of Hasidism which came to rely on excessive use of Kabbalah were quickly considered outside the norm.

The problem to watch out for is precisely those forms of spirituality which give one an easy high. Why? Because people get high, but can't maintain it since it was not

AS IN HEAVEN

worked on. Consequently, they fall lower from when they started and then really get depressed. Once depressed they begin to react to life strangely. If you take an innocent person who is not yet disciplined, who has not yet dedicated his whole life to Torah, and expose him to such a high dose of mystical truth you will burn him out.

That is essentially what happened with the Jewish People and the Golden Calf. There was no greater manifestation of G–d in history — no greater mystical experience — than the revelation of G–d on Mount Sinai. But they did not utilize the revelation properly. Actually, we need look no further than the Kabbalah-based movement of the false messiah Shabbatai Tzvi. People were exposed to the Kabbalah before they were ready. They couldn't handle it. Of course, they thought they could. The intentions of some of them may even have been good, but history bears out the tragedy of their movement. There is a tremendous power in the mystical experience, but like nuclear energy if it is not utilized properly it becomes a destructive force. Kabbalah is a live wire.

In recent years interest in Judaism has skyrocketed. This resurgence has taken many forms. Many such people who return are immediately struck by the problem just articulated: they are nowhere near the preconditions for learning Kabbalah, mysticism, etc. — which is what they crave. Yet, they need more than just a dry compendium of "Thou shalts" and "Thou shalt nots." For them, certain Hasidic teachings are very good, in my opinion. They help people

SO ON EARTH

understand some of the depth behind the lifestyle. But Hasidism is not the same as Kabbalah.

In any event, be careful when you come out of the ark and discover a new world before you. Whatever you set your heart to first will have the broadest possible ramifications for your future. Before you start "planting vineyards" think about what you are doing. Wine is nice, and has its place. However, the staples must be planted first. A person must be grounded before he sets about building castles.

CHAPTER 18

The Generation Of The Tower

- *Explaining the difference between the Generation of the Flood and the Generation of the Tower, the final redemption missed, the deeper implications of the confrontation between Nimrod and Abraham; and the message of Abraham, the Jewish people, and the entire book.*

And it was that the entire earth was one language, and of one speech. And it came to pass, as they journeyed from the east, that they found a plain in the land of Shinar; and they dwelt there ... (Genesis 11:1-2)

We have already spoken briefly about the Generation of the Tower[121] (which in Hebrew we call the "Generation of Dispersion," *dor haflaga*, because they were ultimately "dispersed" into seventy languages) and contrasted them to the Generation of the Flood, the first ten generations from Adam to Noah. The sins of these first ten generations —

theft, immorality, murder — were rooted in the idea of excessive worship of the individual: the individual desire, the individual impulse, the individual whim, etc. In essence, they denied heaven: they denied any obligation to a higher calling, a calling larger than their individual desires.

The essential sin of the latter ten generations — from Noah to Abraham, and culminating in the Generation of Dispersion — was the diametric opposite. They set out to build the Tower of Babel at the expense of all individuality. If a man died during the building process they paid no attention, but if a stone fell they cried over the great loss. The Tower became the State — the Center toward which all individuals gave up their individuality in order to perpetuate its existence. In essence, they denied the earth: the human part, the part of each of us that has individual desires. Earthly, individual, human desires can be harnessed for good. If you cut yourself off from the earthly material you were given to harness, then you frustrate the purpose of creation.[122]

The human ideal is to unite heaven and earth. The Generation of the Flood denied heaven. The Generation of Dispersion denied earth (without necessarily accepting heaven either, as we shall see). Both extremes frustrated the purpose of creation, and when the negative tendencies and lifestyles of these generations spiraled out of control, beyond any hope of correction, both generations had to be dealt with accordingly.

🍎 AS IN HEAVEN

Final Redemption Missed

However, it did not have to be so. In fact, at the time of the Generation of Dispersion the world was ripe for its final redemption. They were united like never before.

> "And the entire world was of one language, and one [common] interest [*devarim achadim*, i.e. to build the Tower] ... and each man said to his friend [i.e. there was a spirit of community] ... 'Come, let *us* [*lanu*] build a city ... and let us make a name for *us* [*lanu*]...' " (Genesis 11:1-4)

There was no talk of "me." It was always *lanu*, "us." They preached the communist ideal. (See Chapter 15.) There was one leader (Nimrod), one language, one common goal. And, in theory at least, they possessed the potential to use that unity in the service of repairing the world shattered into fragmentation by the first man, Adam.

They did not, of course. In fact, they became known as the Generation of Dispersion, forever serving as a symbol for the exact opposite of unification. And we need to learn the lesson of their failure because the fabric of our society, too, is threatening to fall apart. The breakdown of the family, violence, crime, etc. — the center is crumbling. In order to overcome the forces of dispersion rampant in our time we would do well to seek an understanding of the dynamics behind the failure of the Generation of Dispersion.

SO ON EARTH

Making a Name for Themselves

When the Torah tells us: "And it was that the entire earth was one language. . ." it is informing us that humanity at that time was in the deepest way ripe for synthesizing heaven and earth. Language is the paradigm of unity. In order to articulate, a human being must combine two opposites: body and soul. Bodily parts (the throat, tongue, lips, etc.) must be coordinated to move in unison with thought (a prime soul quality). Intelligent, human speech, therefore, is the point where body and soul touch. The human being, the speaker, is the bridge. He has the potential to connect the soul with the body.

If the entire generation was "of one language," then they possessed the ability to synthesize heaven (the soul) and earth (the body). What was their downfall? They reversed the order: they did not want to make earth a mirror image of heaven, but heaven a mirror image of earth!

> And they said, "Come, let us build a city and a tower, whose top reaches into heaven, and make a name for *ourselves*. . ." (Genesis 11:4)

They built the Tower *not* to make a name for G–d, but for *themselves*. They had ideals, but their own man-made ideals. A person who fashions his own ideals, like a fashioner of idols, is making G–d into his image rather than making himself into G–d's image! The Tower therefore was intended as a substitute for the *absence* of G–d, not as a sanctuary for the *presence* of G–d. (The phrase, "And it came to pass as they journeyed from the *east,"* is interpreted by the Sages of the *Midrash*: "... they journeyed from the *primordial One*," i.e. G–d.[123])

The attitude of the generation was epitomized in the name of their leader Nimrod. The root letters of "Nimrod" mean "to rebel." And indeed although he preached unity his intentions were not holy; rather they were to unify the generation in rebellion against G–d.

During that same generation Abraham was coming into maturity. (He was forty-eight years old at the time of the dispersion.) While Nimrod represented the body, Abraham represented the soul. The purpose of the body is to perform the will of the soul. In fact, the body is elevated when used in service of the soul. Had Nimrod made himself subservient to Abraham, then body and soul would have existed in perfect unity. Heaven and earth would have been in beautiful harmony. Nimrod and his generation, however, did not want to be subservient. They were unified, but in rebellion against G–d.

Nimrod therefore imprisoned Abraham and tried to get him to renounce his belief in the one, true G–d. Then he threw Abraham into a furnace (from which he was miraculously saved). The body of the generation insisted on dominating the soul. That is the diametric opposite of what is necessary to bring about the proper synthesis of heaven and earth.

SO ON EARTH

Breaking Away

This explains the continuation of the story, when G–d tells Abraham to "go away from your land, from your birthplace, from the house of your father" (12:1). The society, the institutions — the body — of the generation had become instruments of oppression. They were tools of perpetuating the establishment — and its upside-down order — rather than vehicles for creating a new earth in perfect harmony with the designs of heaven. Abraham — representing the soul quality of the generation — had become an alien, an outcast, a wanderer. The institutions did not recognize him, did not give his voice ascendancy, did not even give him the opportunity for expression or expansion. The soul of the world was without a body. Consequently, that soul — Abraham — had to begin the process of making his own communal-societal body which would enable his soul to become manifest on the earth. Abraham therefore had to go away from "his country, his birthplace, his father's house" in order to find himself, in order to create an alternate body, an alternate vehicle, for his message.

That is what the rest of the Book of Genesis is about: how Abraham became first a father, and then a grandfather, and finally a forefather, of a body of people through whom his message would pulse. And that is where we stand today: a world still waiting for the intellect and spirit of Abraham to become fully manifest.

Abraham's message did not and does not entail denying heaven. Neither did he tell people to deny earth — to deny

AS IN HEAVEN

their material needs and individuality. His message was to restore the order that would enable heaven and earth to work as one unit — like the mind and the tongue when they work in unison to produce intelligent speech. His message is that we must try to align the earth into becoming a mirror image of heaven. This was Abraham's mission, and this is the mission of the people who came to embody his essence.

As in heaven, so on earth. This is the message.

SUPPLEMENT A

The Creation Of Elokim

- *Explaining why the seventy-two Jewish sages intentionally mistranslated the Torah into Greek.*

The Torah begins: *Beraishis bara Elokim*, which is usually translated: "In the beginning G–d created." According to the literal order in which the words appear, though, the translation more properly reads: "In the beginning created G–d (*Elokim*)." This rendition was so prone to misinterpretation that when seventy-two Jewish sages were put in separate rooms to translate the Torah into Greek by King Ptolmey they all uniformly translated: *Elokim bara beraishis*, "G–d (*Elokim*) created the beginning."[124] The reason they translated that way was, as incredible as it sounds, the literal word order — *Beraishis bara Elokim* — implies that G–d (*Elokim*) was a creation!

❦ AS IN HEAVEN

The actual word order, of course, is not a mistake or an accident. It teaches a profound and subtle truth, namely that *Hashem* — G–d in His most transcendent, essential nature — created creation. However, in so doing He also, so to speak, "created" *Elokim*, i.e. He created "G–d" *in the aspect of* relating to creation. Without creation there is no *Elokim*; this aspect of G–d is not manifest. In that sense it can be said that *Elokim* is a "creation."

Of course, in reality, G–d Himself is above creation and in no way reducible to any aspect of creation. Yet, for our sake He constricts Himself so that we — His creations — may relate to Him on some level. That is *Elokim*, the G–d known to all creation.

The verse does not, therefore, teach that G–d was a creation. It merely means to convey that everything in creation can relate to G–d at least on some level. G–d, however, in His truest sense is beyond the natural grasp of human understanding. In actuality, then, the literal translation of our Torah is very precise and teaches us a beautiful nuance: G–d as *Elokim* can be comprehended by all.

To the pagan, Greek-speaking world, however, such a nuance would have been misinterpreted to reducing G–d *in His entirety* to nothing more than a comprehensible element of creation like everything else in creation. Such a reduction would ultimately make Him not as All-Powerful as the Torah clearly understands Him to be. For that reason the distortion had to be perpetrated.

SUPPLEMENT B

The Twilight Zone

- *Explaining the events of twilight, the quality of twilight, and the power of being human.*

Our Sages teach that ten things were created during the twilight (*bain hashmashos*) at the end of the sixth day.[125] Among them are the grave of Moses, the crevice in the earth which swallowed Korach and his followers, the mouth of the donkey which spoke to Bilaam, the ram which Abraham slaughtered in place of his son, etc. What is the meaning of this enigmatic teaching? And what do the creation of these things have to do with twilight?

Twilight

All life is one, large interconnected unity. Therefore, if you find two things which seemingly have no connection to each other, in actuality there must be some link, some bridge. Consequently, if you find, on one hand, the concept of six days and the mundane next to, on the other hand, the

AS IN HEAVEN

seventh day and the divine you must also be able to find a linking concept, something that shares aspects of both but is actually neither.

This is twilight.

Twilight is the bridge, the link. Everything that came to be during twilight of the sixth day was something with universal repercussions which blended elements of the holy and the mundane, the Sabbath and the weekday, the eternal and the time-bound, the Divine and the human. Thus, for instance, when G–d saw ahead of time that one day Korach would choose to rebel against Moses[126] He created the crevice into which Korach and his followers would be swallowed. That crevice would never have been created had not Korach used his free will to rebel against G–d. But G–d saw beforehand that Korach would use his free will for evil and thus brought the crevice into existence.[127] *The crevice was created during twilight because it was a combined human and Divine effort.*[128]

To bring another example, consider the ram which Abraham slaughtered in place of his son, Yitzchak. G–d saw beforehand that Abraham would stand up to this test of tests — Abraham's tenth test — and so He created the ram *in response* to the future efforts of Abraham which He foresaw. The ram was a combined effort, in other words: a combined effort between Abraham and G–d.

Korach used his free will for evil; Abraham used it for good. Similarly, among the list of items created at twilight some resulted from good and others from bad. The

SO ON EARTH

common denominator is that each reflected something monumental and came about as the result of some combination between good and evil, holy and mundane.

Creating Your Own Reality

There is a great practical lesson from all this: human actions have the power to create good or evil. In many ways, we create our own reality for better or worse. True, if one wants one can always pin the blame on others, be it G–d, the government, his neighbor, etc. The truth, however, is that reality responds in great part to our initiative.

This, of course, does not exclude the fact that G–d is the Creator, the only Creator. As the first of the Thirteen Principles of Faith states: "He did, does, and will do all things that come to pass." (See Chapter 3.) We do not do anything in that respect. Nevertheless, G–d granted human beings a unique power: the power to initiate, to choose a direction we want to go. And it is from this choice of direction, this power of initiation, that subsequent reality flows. We are therefore literally our own worst enemies or our own best friends. In either scenario the lesson is that an enormous amount of power has been deposited into our hands to create the reality of the world we live in.

Life: One Great Twilight Period

When we use our power of free will for evil we create the vehicles of our own destruction, as Korach did; we seed the evil which will become manifest sooner or later.[129] However, when we use this power for good, then life becomes a bridge from the sixth days into the Sabbath, from the mundane into the holy, from the physical into the spiritual.

This helps explain why, for instance, it is considered meritorious to take on the Sabbath a little earlier than sundown of Friday night (*tosfos Shabbos*). This act is actually symbolic of the idea that we can take the twilight and sanctify it. Twilight, this mixed potential — this in-between state — can be converted entirely to good. We do that by turning twilight of late Friday afternoon into the sanctified and sublime atmosphere of the holy Sabbath.

In the broadest sense, our entire life is one great twilight period. It is a time of opportunity to create a bridge between the earthly and the heavenly, the weekday and the Sabbath, the "this-worldly" and the "next-worldly." A meaningful life is measured according to the success one transforms every time-bound activity of the weekday world into a bridge that leads directly into the timeless eternal reality which is the Sabbath. That bridge is our product. It is our share in the partnership that our Creator privileged us with.

SO ON EARTH

References

1. See Chapter 5 about becoming a partner with G–d.
2. See Rashi to verse 1, quoting the *Midrash*.
3. *Tanna D'bei Eliyahu*, beginning.
4. *Avos* 1:12.
5. *Beraishis Rabbah* 24:7.
6. Archeologists can attest that this has always been one of the hallmarks of the Jewish People. When they conduct their digs they frequently come upon old graveyards. Almost invariably, they immediately recognize which was a Jewish burial site by the way the bones were buried. If the remains seemed to have been left in an ordered, respectful fashion, then that cues them into the fact that it is probably a Jewish cemetery.
7. "... be fruitful and multiply, and *fill* the earth and conquer it" (Genesis 1:28). Our purpose is to "fill" the hollow wherever G-d's presence seems to be lacking. Our job is to recognize G-d's presence. Doing so fixes the lack; it fills the hollow.
8. See *Choose Life!*, the essay on *Rosh HaShannah: Unveiling The Purpose Of Creation*.
9. See *I Shall Not Want*.
10. This is why "And G–d said, Let us make man..." is the tenth of the Ten Sayings. (See Chapter 10.)
11. *Avos* 5:1.
12. *Megillah* 21b.
13. *Beraishis Rabbah* 1:2.
14. That is why the ten sayings begin with the letter *bais* (the *bais* of *beraishis*, which the Talmud tells us constituted a saying unto itself), the second letter in the Hebrew alphabet, while the Ten Commandments begin with an *alef*, the first letter.

AS IN HEAVEN

15. *Chiddushei HaRim;* the concept can also be found in *Sfas Emes.*
16. *Yoma* 28b.
17. *Sanhedrin* 4:5.
18. *Avos* 3:15.
19. See also Introduction to *I Shall Not Want*, Chapter 3 of *Darkness Before Dawn*, and Chapter 1 of *Beyond Survival*.
20. *Chagigah* 12a.
21. *Chagigah* 12a.
22. See *Choose Life!.*
23. See *Darkness Before Dawn.*
24. Isaiah 42:6.
25. *Beraishis Rabbah* 4:6.
26. And this was the "consolation" for the "lower waters." They would never be absolutely cut off from the purity of their counterpart waters in heaven. This also explains why on the third day when G–d "gathered together the lower waters into one place" the Torah stated *twice* that "it was good" — once for the events of the third day itself and once for the second day, because despite the initial division (which made it untenable to call the day's events "good") the act was ultimately for the good of all.
27. Similarly, what water is for a living person the earth is for a dead person. Putting the body in the ground and letting it decay is essentially the same as immersing oneself in water to affect a cleansing. It is an act of nullification. In terms of the grave this nullification is necessary to correct Adam's sin: "From dust you were made and to dust you shall return." The complete nullification of the physical body through the process of decay earns it the right to be reconstituted and resurrected in the World To Come. Indeed, then, *mikvah* and *kever* (grave) share much in common: both affect a nullification which leads ultimately to a higher state of existence.
28. The Hebrew word for contamination is *tumah.* Halachically speaking, the *mikvah* is the vehicle whereby a Jewish person contaminated with one of the forms of spiritual contamination mentioned in the Torah can cleanse him or herself. The Torah's laws of contamination and purity, *tumah* and *taharah*, are exceedingly complex. At the risk of oversimplifying it, we can nevertheless say that the common denominator of all contamination is loss of potential life. Life is the greatest gift. Wherever a void of life occurs — even through no fault of anyone involved — a vacuum is created for

SO ON EARTH

contamination, or *tumah*, to enter.

For instance, a woman's monthly cycle is designed to bring life into the world. If that cycle passes, if she becomes menstrual, the loss of potential life causes her to become contaminated in the spiritual sense, to acquire *tumah*. A man, too, has to worry about a comparable possibility. His potential to bring life into this world is through semen. If he uses it not as it is intended to be used, then he also acquires a type of spiritual contamination (albeit, not a contamination with the same practical *halachic* ramifications as in the woman's case). He has disconnected himself from potential life, from the heavenly element, and that is an act, whether voluntary or involuntary, which brings about *tumah*, contamination.

29. *Taanis* 7a.
30. *Sefer HaZikronos*.
31. One *amah* is a measurement equal to about two feet (opinions vary). Four *amos* (plural of *amah*) is about eight feet and refers to the circumference of territory surrounding each person.
32. *Berachos* 8a.
33. The Ark was two and a half *amos* long plus one and a half *amos* wide, totally four *amos*.
34. Deuteronomy 20:19.
35. Commentary on Torah.
36. The Ramban explains that G–d created everything in the first instance with the word "*beraishis*." From this undifferentiated, all-inclusive original material He then set about the business of "making" or organizing the rest of creation over the six days.
37. These two human potentials can be seen in the second description of man's creation when the Torah repeats itself in Chapter 2, "And G–d formed man from the dust of the ground and blew into his nostrils the breath of life a living soul. . ." (Gen. 2:7). First G–d formed man from the dust of the ground. That refers to the fourth level of creation, the man whose ultimate connection is to the ground, the earth. Then, G–d blew into him an eternal soul (*nishmas chaim*). This is the element which comes directly from the eternal G–d. It gives the human being a new dimension, a new potential. (See Chapter 10).
38. Rashi to Genesis 6:9.
39. Sanhedrin 90a. Thirteenth of the 13 Principles of Faith (*siddur*); see <u>Beyond Survival</u>, Chapter 8.

40. The world was created with Ten Sayings (*Avos* 5:1); each of Abraham's tests was to see if he was willing to nullify the part of himself reflecting that quality of the physical creation corresponding to each of the Ten Sayings — see Chapter 2.
41. Imagine a person who claims he loves G–d more than anything in the world, that he will do anything G–d says. G–d then says to him, "You say you love me so, that you are willing to do anything I say — well, then do this for me: I want you to exterminate My people." That is exactly the test Abraham was given. His son represented the future of the Jewish people. If he had been killed the entire Jewish people would have been wiped out. Abraham's test, then, was really to dash all his spiritual desires, to destroy everything he had pinned his hope for a revitalized humanity upon, to nullify everything he thought he knew G–d wanted. When he showed he was willing to do so without questions, without hesitation, he proved he was willing to surrender his will for G–d's. In essence, he undid Adam's sin. That was his greatness.
42. See *Likkutei Torah*.
43. *Shabbos* 10a.
44. *Yevamos* 61a, expounding Ezekiel 34:31. "You [Family of Israel] are called Adam. . ."
45. G–d is ultimately transcendent. He is totally outside our capability of understanding. Therefore, when the verse says we are made in the image of G–d it does not refer to the image of the transcendent G–d, of G–d's essence. It is referring to the image of G–d *who created the world* and relates to it in a certain way. This G–d, so to speak, is possible to grasp. And it is the image of this aspect of G–d in which we are made.
46. Genesis 2:18.
47. Psalms 89:3.
48. *Yevamos* 62b. More statements of the Sages regarding the relationship between men and women can be found in the Appendices to *To Become One*.
49. *Sanhedrin* 38b.
50. The truth is that he did have a mate, as the Torah says: "male and female He created them," i.e. Eve was part of his being from the beginning. (See Chapter 6.) However, originally she was literally connected to him. And since they were not yet separate beings they could not really express their full beauty. The male part was not able to express its full masculinity. And the female part was

SO ON EARTH

not able to express its full femininity. The net result is that even though Adam was given his highest soul and the keys to the universe in the sixth hour he was still a creature designated "not good."

51. *Yevamos* 62a; but see *Tosafos, Sanhedrin* 38b.
52. *Nesiv HaTeshuva*.
53. *Berachos* 34b.
54. The letter *mem* represents the physical. The physical is not inherently good or bad. It can be a conduit for good just as easily as it can be a stumbling block for bad. *Alef*, which numerically equals one, represents G–d, who is one. (The *alef* can also be broken down into two *yuds* and a *vav*, which numerically equal twenty-six. Twenty-six in turn equals the numerical value of the four letter name of G–d.) *Dalet*, which numerically equals four, represents the unformed human being. (Also, a *dal* is a poor person.) Four represents a square, or the physical world (the "four corners of the globe"), which is worthless and empty in and of itself. *Dalet* and *mem* are similar in this regard (*mem* [40] is a multiple of *dalet* [4]).

    Tying it all together, the lesson is that a person must start with the *alef*, the Divine, and empty himself out in order to allow the *alef* to flow through his veins. If he does that he will produce a *mem*, a physical life infused with the spiritual, an earthly life that is a conduit for heaven. If, however, he reverses the order and starts out with the *mem* — i.e. he makes the earthly life his first priority — then he is in a state of *meod* (*mem-alef-dalet*), "very." That is what Adam did by not surrendering his will to the divine will. He mixed up the order of his very name and put everything in disarray. Still and all, it was out of this sin — out of this corruption of the original order — that the world was put into the state of "very good," as we have explained in the main text. The possibility of disorder enabled humanity to be the primary partner restoring the world to its original order. "*Meod*" made it possible for Adam to (re)create *alef-dalet-mem*: Adam.
55. See Chapter 13 for an explanation of the real "sin" in Adam's sin.
56. *Koheles* 7:20.
57. *Yoma* 8:9. "One who says, 'I will sin and repent; sin and repent,' will not be given an opportunity to repent."
58. *Beraishis Rabbah* 9:7.
59. *Hateva*, literally "the nature," in numerical terms equals eighty-six, the numerical value of *Elokim*.

❧ AS IN HEAVEN

60. See Exodus 6:2,3. See our discussion in *Darkness Before Dawn*, Chapter 7, subchapter, "Conclusion;" and *Self-Esteem*, essay on *Pesach*, subchapter, "The Self-Replicating Program," and *Beyond Survival*, Chapter 2, "The Creator."
61. *Midrash Rabbah* 12:9.
62. The *bais* (b') is merely a prefix and not part of Abraham's name. Moreover the letter *hey* of *biheebaram* must, according to tradition, be written unusually small. This, too, is a further allusion to the extra *hey* which G–d would add to Abraham's name in his merit.
63. Thus, Rashi answers the difficulty of how the verse here, describing the sixth day, can state: ". . . no grass of the field had yet sprouted," when in fact the Torah already noted the creation of plant life on the third day.
64. Psalms 89:3.
65. *Derech Hashem* 1:2:1.
66. Ibid. 1:2:5.
67. *Taanis* 2a.
68. *Avos* 5:1.
69. The word *vayeetzer*, "formed," in this verse is spelled strangely. Instead of one *yud* (as it is spelled in verse 19 regarding the "formation" of the animals) it has two (*vav, yud, yud, tzadi, raish*). This, too, alludes to the idea that we were created with two parts. On one hand, we have a body and share characteristics with the animal kingdom. That is the first *yud*. (And that is why the word "formed" in verse 19 — the verse about the formation of the animals — has only one *yud*.) The second *yud*, though, relates to something beyond that. It represents the absolute essence of G–dliness, as it is reflected in the G–dly human being. It represents the higher soul.
70. Ramban.
71. *Avos* 5:21.
72. *Avos* 4:16.
73. The verse says: *Olamecha tireh b'chayecha*, "your world, you will see in your life." This world is not really the world. *Olamecha*, your world, is *olam habah*, the World To Come. What does *olam habah* consist of, though? *Chayecha*, your life in this world, *olam hazeh*. *Olamecha tireh b'chayecha* means that those things which you accomplished here in your pre-*olam habah* life (*chayecha*) are the very things you will live off of in your future life (*olamecha*).

SO ON EARTH

74. *Avos* 6:2.
75. See *I Shall Not Want*.
76. See Chapter 6; see also *To Become One*, especially Chapter 4.
77. For instance, he wanted to sin so he could do *teshuva* (see Chapter 7) or he wanted to destroy the world so he could rebuild it (this chapter ahead), or he wanted to exert admirable individuality, etc.
78. By the way, this leads to an important point: If G–d created us with the potential to perpetuate disorder, then He created us with the potential to put everything back in its right spot. The same is true from a personal, individual standpoint as well. Whatever chaos we cause in our personal lives we have the ability to right. Our potential for destruction is not greater than our potential for creation and rebuilding. The two go hand in hand. So, there is no reason to despair no matter how far a person may have sunk.
79. See Chapter 7.
80. *Avos* 1:6.
81. *Pesachim* 8b.
82. This question is asked by Rabbi Meir Simcha HaCohen of Dvinsk in his *Meshech Chochmah*.
83. Ibid.
84. *Beraishis Rabbah* 20:12.
85. *Ayin* and *alef* sound virtually the same. (Today, only the Yemenite dialect makes any real distinction in sound between the two letters.) An *ayin* and *alef* are also composed of the same basic shapes. (If you take the long line on the right side of the *ayin* and "lean" it diagonally to the left, take the *vav*-like other arm of the *ayin*, cut it into two *yuds*, and put them at either end of the long diagonal line you get an *alef*.)
86. Perhaps this is the implication of the verse, "And Shem and Yefes took *the* garment... and covered their father's nakedness" (Gen. 9:23). They did not just take "a" garment, but "the" garment.
87. *Beraishis Rabbah* 63:13.
88. Ibid. 65:16.
89. Ibid.
90. Rashi, Genesis 27:27.
91. Genesis 27:27.
92. Genesis 25:27.
93. Thus, for instance, when Daniel was thrown into the lion's pit they did not touch him because he was a person through whom the *tzelem Elokim* could be discerned. For the same reason when

References 253

Joseph was thrown into the pit, in which there were scorpions and snakes, he was unharmed. His *tzelem Elokim* protected him. His skin was a translucent "garment of light." It let his inner holiness shine through.

94. This could be why some Sages say that Adam's garment was one of the things created during twilight of the first Sabbath (*Pesachim* 54b). See Supplement B for our discussion concerning why twilight epitomizes the idea of time which can be used to either create good or evil.
95. Numbers 23:21.
96. According to the Sages, in a teaching we elaborated upon before (*Sanhedrin* 38b; see Chapter 6), the birth of Cain and Abel apparently took place *before* the sin (yet we first learn about it here, *after* the description of the sin; the Torah does not necessarily tell us events strictly in their chronological order.) The reason it is mentioned now is because the Torah's style is to follow through on one lesson all the way before retracing and detailing a tangent within that lesson. (See also Chapter 8.) Thus, the Torah begins with Adam's story — his creation, his sin, and ultimately his punishment and expulsion from the Garden — before picking up the thread of the lives of Cain and Abel, who were born in the Garden before the sin.
97. Hinted at the description in this verse regarding Cain's conception and birth is the idea we have mentioned previously (Chapter 5), namely that the human ideal is to become a partner with G–d. For the Talmud (*Niddah* 31a) says: "A human being is the product of three partners: G–d, the father, and the mother." Cain's birth marked the first time this partnership was realized. Thus, when Chava named him "Cain" she said, "I have acquired a man *with* G–d." It was an effort between Adam and Chava *with* G–d. Cain's birth, therefore, illustrates the idea that we can strive to become a partner with G–d.
98. *Avos* 1:12.
99. *Sanhedrin* 4:5.
100. Rashi; cf. Kli Yakar.
101. Rashi based on *Sanhedrin* 108a.
102. Proverbs 22:6.
103. Rashi.
104. See Chapter 3.
105. *Shabbos* 104a.

SO ON EARTH

106. Ibid.
107. Psalms 85:12.
108. *Beraishis Rabbah* 34:9.
109. *Daniel*, Chapter 4.
110. *Aitz Yosef.*
111. See the Appendix to *Choose Life!* for a fascinating introductory article on the codes entitled: *Back To The Future.*
112. For example, if *heh-yud-tes-lamed-raish* was located in one place with 50 other letters between each of the five letters of Hitler's name, and in another place with only 20 letters between each of the letters, the 20 letter interval was assumed to be more significant.
113. Thirty-one is highly significant because there are thirty-one Torah prohibitions against speaking *loshon hara* (evil, slanderous speech). *Loshon hara*, literally, "the evil tongue," was the prime ingredient of the sin of the snake in the Garden of Eden. It used its slithering tongue to bring about sin, destruction, and death to the world. As is well-known, Hitler's one real talent was his ability to persuade others through speech. He was a fiery orator who induced an entire continent to sin grievously and bring about destruction and death. In all likelihood, probably only the primal snake, who induced all of humankind extant in its day to sin grievously, can be said to have been more destructive.
114. The timing of the latter three's sacrifice is significant. They lived at the beginning of the Babylonian exile, the first of the four exiles the Jewish people would have to endure. Their self-sacrifice and devotion therefore served as a flag for Jews of all the ensuing exiles who would have to face life and death choices.
115. See <u>Darkness Before Dawn</u>, for a full treatment of this theme, and especially Chapter 5.
116. *Sanhedrin* 59b.
117. Rashi, Genesis 9:4, based on *Sanhedrin* 59.
118. *Sanhedrin* 108a.
119. Later (9:22-23) after Noah was "naked in his tent," Shem and Yefes took a garment and covered him. The Sages tell us that as a reward for this meritorious act each of their descendants became worthy of a particular reward (*Beraishis Rabbah* 36:6). The descendants of Yefes would be worthy of burial after they are killed in the apocalyptic war of "Gog and Magog" (*Ezekiel* 39:11). In other words, just as their forefather Yefes covered Noah, so too would

AS IN HEAVEN

they be worthy to not have their bodies rot in the open, but to be buried. While meritorious, Yefes's act was motivated by a superficial sense of human dignity. Consequently, his descendants will be rewarded in a superficial sense.

Shem, on the other hand, was motivated by true, internal reasons, as we will see ahead. His reward, the Sages tell us, was that his descendants would be given the commandment of *tzitzis* (the four-cornered garment). *Tzitzis* symbolize the entire Torah. Shem's reward, then, matches his act. Since he was motivated from a genuine source he was rewarded with people who would be given Torah. (And Torah, ultimately, is the secret to the "resurrection of the dead." Yefes's descendants, on the other hand, were given dignified graves, not the keys to eternal life. His externally motivated act merited him a superficial reward; Shem's internally motivated act merited his genuine reward.)

120. *Niddah* 30b.
121. Chapter 15.
122. The Zohar illustrates this idea in a profound and beautiful fashion. The word *hashamayim*, "the heaven," has virtually the same letters as the word *neshama*, "soul." The difference (other than the order of the letters) is that whereas *hashamayim* is spelled with a *yud* and a *mem*, the word *neshama* is spelled with a *nun*. (This is not a significant difference since the numerical value of *yud* plus *mem* [50] equals the numerical value of *nun* [50].) The idea is as follows: The letter *mem* represents earthly, physical nature. That is why its shape is square, like a box, which means that it has limits; it has dimension. *Yud*, on the other hand, is essentially a dot, the smallest possible mark, and therefore represents transcendence, spirituality.

A human being comes into this world possessing side-by-side these two elements: *yud* and *mem*. He has the spiritual element, the *yud*, and the physical element, the *mem*. *The object of life is to merge them into one unit,* to merge the *yud* and *mem* into one. Merging a *yud* (heaven) and *mem* (earth) into one produces *nun* (soul). And that is the goal: to transform the latent, raw spirituality of *hashamayim*, "the heaven," into the actualized potential of *neshama*, "soul."

123. *Beraishis Rabbah* 38:7.
124. *Megillah* 9a. This is why it seems like such a natural translation today. The Greek translation, which became known as the

SO ON EARTH

Septuagint, or the "Translation of the Seventy (Sages)," became the standard Christian translation. From the Septuagint later came the Latin translation (Vulgate) from which eventually came the English translation (King James version). Thus, what seems like a natural translation is in reality a distortion originally set in motion by seventy-two Jewish Sages who each knew independently that the literal translation would prove problematic to the pagan, Greek-speaking world.

125. *Avos* 5:6.
126. *Numbers*, Chapter 16.
127. This is not a contradiction between free will and foreknowledge. (In fact, this is one of the ways of answering that paradox.) Korach had free will. G–d's foreknowledge of his future choices did not interfere with his ability to choose. Therefore, G–d was able to create the crevice at twilight at the end of the sixth day of creation long before Korach's rebellious actions and yet in response to his actions.
128. The universal repercussion was rebelling against Moses, the teacher of Torah, at a time when his authority was still somewhat vulnerable to challenge.
129. Thus, according to some Sages quasi-spiritual, quasi-physical destroying spirits or demons were also amongst the things created at twilight. *Avos* 5:6.

AUDIO TAPES BY RABBI EZRIEL TAUBER

The following is a partial listing of tapes in English by Rabbi Ezriel Tauber, including lectures through the Summer of 5755. Also available are tapes in Hebrew, Yiddish, and Russian, as well as videos (see end of list). Prices are $4.00 per tape and $15.00 per video (plus shipping and handling). Visa and Mastercard accepted. For further information contact:

Shalheves
P.O. Box 361
Monsey, NY 10952
Phone: 914-356-3515
Fax: 914-425-2094
Orders: 1-800-998-0400

EMUNAH & BITACHON

26	13 Principles Of Faith By The Rambam
241	Who Am I?
323	Should We Plan?
782	Believing In Hashem
799	The Full Emunah
832	The First Principal Of Belief
1223	Believing
1292	Bitachon In Stressful Situations
1368	Applying Bitachon To Our Daily Struggles
1434	First Aid For Worriers
1445	Real Bitachon
1457	Finding Hashem When We Feel Alone
1541	The Need Of Bitachon Today
1565	Bitachon Is The Answer
1587	Money Covers Everything
1594	How To Practice Bitachon (Advanced)
1625	Belief In The Darkness
1645	The Definition Of Belief (A-E)
1654	Survival Today
1685	The Reality Of G–D
1686	Mitzvas Yichud Hashem
1693	How To Develop Faith
1695	Suffering Develops Faith
1696	Emunah In Practical Life
1700	Knowledge & Faith — Two Sides Of One Coin
1737	Develop Belief Into Knowledge
1751	Three Steps In Belief
1785	Overcoming The Fear Of Change
1825	Belief Vs. Fanaticism
1856	Never Ever Despair
1881	Philosophy Or Faith
1888	The Power Of Faith
1890	How To Manage Stress In Life
1911	Chizuk

THE PURPOSE OF CREATION

144	The Tree Which Is A Fruit
518	The Purpose Of Creation
519	Yisroel — Fulfillment Of Creation
607	Life In Gan Eden
821-A	The Meaning Of Life — A
821-B	The Meaning Of Life — B
1098	Creation And It's Purpose
1338	A Time For Renewal
1438	Us In Creation
1586-A	The Jew And The World — A
1586-B	The Jew And The World — B
1722	The Process Of Creation
1896	Nature Vs. Miracle

THE JEWISH NATION

269	Should We Isolate Or Integrate
316	The Structure Of The Jewish Nation
648	The Jewish Nations Responsibility To The World

AUDIO TAPES
BY RABBI EZRIEL TAUBER

758 The Definition Of A Jewish Nation — A
758 The Benefit Of Suffering — B
796 Be A Proud Jew
805 My Share In The World To Come
872 Know G–D — A
872 Our Crucial Days — B
900 Let's Build Am Yisroel
901 Be Aware Of Your Duties
959 Leaving Egypt Today
1455 Are We Chosen?
1497 We — As Hashem's Ambassadors
1673 Live A Whole Life
1726 The Meaning Of Being Chosen
1898 Jewish Survival
1915 Truth Is The Foundation

THE VALUE OF LIFE

170 Life After Death
176 Is There Everyday Life?
201 Purpose Of Life (Part 1)
202 Mysticism In Everyday Life (Part 2)
203 Mysticism In Everyday Life (Part 3)
295 Real Life
818 The Value Of Life
903 Definition Of Truth And The Essence Of Life
997 Every Inch Of Life — Ongoing Bliss To Avodas Hashem
1000 The Value Of A Moment
1008 Every Moment A Mission To Hashem
1029 Is There Freedom Of Choice?
1073 Positive Speech
1101 Destiny Of Life
1154 Value Of A Moment Of Life
1218 How To Grow Every Minute
1242 The Ultimate Goal
1243 The Real Free Choice
1315 Appreciate Life
1316 Appreciate Life
1330 The Meaning Of Life
1340 Find Meaning In Life
1376 The Value Of Life
1452 Two Parts Of Life
1489 To Live For Now
1668 The Foundation Of Life
1682 The Value Of Life
1704 The Value Of Life
1774 The Value Of Life
1802 Living Each Day
1905 Life After Life
1942 The Value Of Life
1958 The Quality Of Life
1960 Multiplication Of Life

THE MEANING OF A JEW

241 Who Am I?
640 Live With Confidence
690 Effort Of Competition
1380 Meaning Of A Jew
1578 My Greatness
1579 I — The Original Jew
1581 Avrohom — Today
1731 How Judaism Developed
1806 The Relationship Between G–D And A Jew, And G–D And A Non-Jew
1900 Guard Your Tongue
1901 The Secret Of Jew
1904 Be A Happy Jew
1908 If You Choose Me — Than I Choose You
1970 Your Greatness

THE GREATNESS OF MAN

670 All Israel Has A Share In The World To Come
737 Love Your Friend As Yourself
753 Discover Yourself
902 How Hashem Tells Me What To Do
913 Ner Hashem Nishmas Adam
945 The Meaning Of The Image Of Hashem
1280 I, As The Only Man On The Planet
1322 You Come First
1333 The Greatness Of Man
1431 You Can Be A Prophet
1753 How Important We Are
1762 Respect Yourself
1781 Your Role In The World
1807 Growing Each Day
1855 Have Self Respect
1871 How To Develop Respect
1879 The Formation Of Man

AUDIO TAPES
BY RABBI EZRIEL TAUBER

1918	Building Self Esteem	1804	Have We Fulfilled Our Role In Golus
1963	Discover Yourself		
1968	Respect Of Man	1870	The Challenge Of Today

HAPPINESS

AHAVAS YISROEL

544	A Happy Life	943	Veahavta Lereacha Komocha
552	Enrich Your Life	988	Ahavas Yisroel
691	Stay High — Always	1077	Chesed To Yourself
789	The Real Simcha	1120	Sensitivity To Peoples Needs
820	Plant Life	1230	How To Love A Jew
836	A Moment Of Life	1298	Being Thankful
951	Appreciate Your Role	1658	To Love Your Fellow Jew
1003	The Meaning Of Happiness	1803	Achdus — The Power Of Unity
1018	Search For Happiness		
1093	Finding Strength	1815	Our Final Test
1119	Finding Strength	1923	Love Your Fellow Man
1502	A Life Which Is All Good		
1532	Torah As A Map		WAITING FOR MOSHIACH
1736	Please Ask Why		
1935	How To Develop Happiness	243	Our Share In Moshiach
		822	Crucial Times Of Today
	THE BENEFIT OF SUFFERING	823	Our Days Of Moshiach
		1070	Days Of Moshiach
554	Suffering As Currency	1082	How To Prepare For Our Times
688	Thank Hashem For Everything		
909-A	Sufferings And Tests During The Times Of Moshiach — A	1128	Our Crucial Days
		1133	How To Wait For Moshiach
909-B	Sufferings And Tests During The Times Of Moshiach — B	1136	Our Times In Depth
		1142	Times For Action
952	Suffering As A Currency	1149	What Are We Really Waiting For
995	Carrying Diamonds		
1100-A	Golus, The Benefit Of Suffering — A	1153	Waiting For Moshiach
		1157	My Share In Moshiach
1100-B	Golus, The Benefit Of Suffering — B	1437	Are We Ready For Moshiach?
		1461	We, In Making Moshiach
1107	How To Accept A Loss In The Family	1656	Our Crucial Days
		1788	Build Your Temple
1129	Our Life As A Plant	1805-A	Tisha B'av — The Birth Of Moshiach
1169	You As An Artist		
1300	The Benefit Of Suffering	1805-B	The Torah Of Moshe & Rabbi Akiva
1328	"Golus", The Benefit Of Suffering		
		1857	The Final Test
1413	Chizuk In Stressful Situations		
1441	The Benefit Of Suffering		PARNASSA
1547	How To Accept Our Challenging Days		
		93	Business And Torah
1727	In Memory Of A Young Adult	167	Business And Torah
1738	How To Deal In Times Of Adversity	232	Bitachon Vs. Effort
		523	Effort And Bitachon
1740	Earn Your Gift	558	The Manna Of Today
1782	Understanding Suffering		

AUDIO TAPES BY RABBI EZRIEL TAUBER

906	Effort And Bitachon Towards Parnassa		1031	Chinuch And Tznius
953-A	Reliance And Effort — A		1590	Parents As Role Models
953-B	Reliance And Effort — B		1599	The Method Of Education
1106	Finding Hashem In Business		1698	The Parents Role In Finding The Right Shidduch
1246	The Man In Nature		1707	The Challenge Of Raising Young Adults
1274	Torah In Business			
1439	Tranquillity In Business		1717	The Final Solution Or Resolution?
			1820	What Is Responsibility?

TESHUVA

188	Our Responsibility Towards The World
250	New Time Of Teshuva
258-A	The Teshuva Prophecy Realized — A
258-B	The Teshuva Prophecy Realized — B
1850	Let's Make Up With Hashem

TEFILLAH

772	An Effective Prayer
1102	Depth Of Tefillah
1551	The Power Of Tefillah
1558	How To Pray
1595	How Prayer Works (Part 1) (Advanced)
1596	How Prayer Works (Part 2) (Advanced)
1752	Principles Of Prayer And Resurrection
1891	How To Ask Hashem

LOSHON HARA

837	I, As A Messenger
1240	Why Loshon Hara?

CHINUCH

101	A Lecture To Teachers Of Girls
740	"Chinuch" — The Real Way
960	When Children Question Our Values
1006-A	Chinuch-The Courage To Say No — A
1006-B	Chinuch — The Courage To Say No — B
1014	Chinuch For Yourself
1030	The Right Chinuch

MARRIAGE

1209	Harmony In The Home I
1210	Harmony In The Home II
1236	How Marriage Helps Us Realize Our Potential
1440	The Torah Concept Of Marriage
1512	For Kallahs
1655	The Foundation Of Marriage
1699	Lecture To Kallahs
1810	The Role Of Man And Woman
1933	Why Man Must Be Married
1949	Peace Starts With You

FOR MEN

618	The Man's Role In A Jewish Family
1080	Lecture For Chassanim (5 Parts) A–E
1550	Man's Role In Marriage
1559	For Men Only
1597	The Man's Role In Marriage
1796	The Man's Role In Klal Yisroel

FOR WOMEN

100	In The Merit Of Righteous Women We Were Redeemed
307	Jewish Concept Of Woman
546	Kiddush Hashem By Women
613	The Woman's Role In The Family
620	"Man And Woman He Created Them"
623	The Woman's Role In Judaism
625	A Happy Jewish Family
651	Woman's Role In Building The Bais Hamikdash
1087	Lecture For Kallahs

AUDIO TAPES
BY RABBI EZRIEL TAUBER

1296	The Meaning Of Marriage	1288	Sarah's Life All Good (Chayai Sarah)
1304	The Woman's Role In Marriage	1493	The Man As A Tree (Bereishis)
1598	The Woman's Role In Marriage	1495	Akaidas Yitzchok Today (Vayaira)
1779	Are Women Discriminated By Halacha?	1506	Yaakov Tricks Eisav, Why?
1784	The Role Of A Woman	1508	Yaakov Vs. Eisav
1797	The Woman's Role In The Jewish Nation	1509	How To Ask Hashem (Toldos)
		1549	Mishpotim
		1556	Build Me A Sanctuary (Truma)
		1564	Half Shekel Or Golden Calf (Ki Sisa)

FOR GIRLS

108	For A Girl — Leaving Egypt	1602	No Reason To Fear (Shlach)
709	Role Of A Jewish Girl	1603	The Spies Of Today
845	Let's Care For Each Other (3 Weeks)	1605	The Only Medicine Today (Shlach)
1057	My Role In Creation	1608	Parshas Shlach
1135	Appreciate Being Chosen	1611	Not To Be Like Korach — Today
1374	For The Seminary Girl		
1702	Chesed Of A Bas Yisroel	1614	Parshas Chukas
1913	You Choose G–D	1852	Introduction To Torah (Bereishis)
		1854	The Sin Of Adam Harishon (Advanced)

PARSHA

Parsha Series — 70 tapes, more in progress. (See ahead, the Section titled TAPE SERIES, for details.)

		1868	The Test Of The Akaida (Vayeira)
		1869	The Tenth Test (Vayeira)
80	Parshas Bereishis	1922	Amalek Against You (Beshalach)
95	Parshas Vayechi		
119	Parshas Yisro — Mishpotim	1927	The Gift Of The Ten Commandments (Yisro)
153	Parshas Vayeitsei		
168	Be Like Ephraim And Menasha (Vayechi)	1940	Fight Your Amalek (Ki Sisa)
192	Make Your Own Luchos (Ki Sisa)		

MISCELLANEOUS

195	Women's Participation In Building Of The Mishkan (Pekudai)	266	The Role Of Our Mother Rachel
		517-A	The Definition Of Truth — A
245	Listen And Then Realize (R'ah)	517-B	The Definition Of Truth — B
		557	Should We Be Exposed To The World?
635	The Bush Burning In Fire (Va'ara)	630	Fashion — The Uniform Of A Goy
666	Benefits Of The Jewish Dietary Laws (Shmini)	632	Multiple Plans In The Universe
695	Parshas Hameraglim (Shlach)	752	Love Hashem
921	Yaakov's Purchase Of Esav's Bechorah (Toldos)	755	Curiosity — Why?
		787	To Combat Proudness
1283	Know Who You Are (Va'yaira)	833	One Solution For All Problems
1286	The Significance Of The Binding Of Yitzchok (Vayaira)	840	Live For The Present
		847	Discover Your Wisdom

AUDIO TAPES
BY RABBI EZRIEL TAUBER

851	Questions And Answers	1671	Could A Holocaust Happen Without G–D?
857	The Meaning Of Chesed		
863	Tranquillity	1674	Mitzvas Yichud Hashem (Advanced)
907	Prophecies In Our Times		
915	Questions And Answers	1675	How To Enjoy Every Moment
927	Money As Eternity	1676	Eretz Yisroel Is Acquired Through Pain
944	We As Survivors		
948	Develop The Right Desire	1742	Men's Development
964	You Cannot Dilute The Truth	1763	Reconciling The Physical And The Spiritual
966-A	Codes In The Torah — A		
966-B	Codes In The Torah — B	1771	Understanding Tfillin According To The Maharal
967	Prophecies Materialized In Our Times		
		1775	Prophesy Fulfillment In Our Days
1021	Achievement Of Positive Thinking		
		1776	Questions And Answers
1094	Getting Things Done	1777	You As A Product Of Miracle
1097	The Definition Of Truth	1778	Questions And Answers
1148	Honoring Parents	1787	Questions And Answers
1185	Questions & Answers	1791	Two Levels In Judaism
1187	Justify Your Consumption	1798	Questions And Answers
1190	Questions & Answers	1808	Definition Of Tznius (Modesty)
1211	Remembering		
1321	How To Find A Friend	1809	Mitzvas Yichud Hashem (Advanced)
1341-A	Codes In The Torah — A		
1341-B	Codes In The Torah — B	1811	Prophecies And Codes In The Torah
1412	Think Right		
1449	Thoughtfulness — Patch Of Relationships	1814	Questions And Answers
		1822	Questions And Answers
1451	Let's Start Thinking	1841	The Theory Of Relativity In The Maharal
1460	Free Will Vs. Fate		
1511	The Real Reason For Anti-Semitism	1853	Derech Eretz Before Torah
		1864	Questions And Answers
1520	Three Conditions To Chassidus	1867	Ask Questions
		1877	Questions And Answers
1522	Questions And Answers	1882	Questions And Answers
1527	How To Acquire Chassidus	1887	Questions And Answers
1542	The Ladder Of Shovevim	1892	Questions And Answers
1543	Holocaust And Zionism	1920	Questions And Answers
1544	Learning The Truth From False	1926	How To Accept The Loss Of A Child
1545	Chizuk	1929	Gratitude
1546	The Importance Of Unity	1931	Questions And Answers
1580	Self Discover Truth	1934	Questions And Answers
1592	Find Your Greatness In Your Nothingness	1939	Questions And Answers
		1944	Our Duty Today
1600	Know How Important You Are	1945	Our Gains From The Holocaust
1609	Questions And Answers		
1612	Why Not To Seek Help By Mystics	1973	The Beauty Of Shabbos
1634	Ten Steps To Growth		
1638	Recapture Yourself		
1670	The Value Of A Moment		

AUDIO TAPES BY RABBI EZRIEL TAUBER

PESACH

207	Do Not Rebel Against The Nations
209	The Four Parshiyos
654	Belief And Knowledge
659	Be Aware Of Our Times
661	Split Your Own Sea
796	Be A Proud Jew
797	Egypt In Our Times
979	Enthusiasm For Pesach
1170	Leaving Egypt Today
1180	Our Crucial Days
1317	Self Appreciation
1381	Uplifting Pesach Thoughts
1392	Celebrate Your Birthday
1568	Pesach
1723	The Process Of Growth
1730	Why To Be A Jew
1734	The Meaning Of Eternity
1735	The Meaning Of Pesach
1955	My Birthday (Pesach)
1957	Me, As A Diamond

SEFIRAS HA'OMER

48	Are You Proud To Be A Jew?
110	Sefira, In Our Time
226	Humility — An Ingredient To Happiness
543	Responsibility — Collectively And Individually
678	Rabbi Akiva's Disciples
810	To Be High — Or Money
819	The Real World
993	Victorious Israel
1186	My Personal Growth
1192	We, As Rabbi Akiva's Talmidim
1398	The Message Of Rabbi Akiva
1585	My Mission
1962	Count Yourself
1964	Become Great
1967	49 Facets In You

SHAVUOS

220	Creation At Matan Torah
317	To Appreciate Our Role
524	The Marriage Of Israel And Hashem
646	Shira Before Torah
682	Let's Do And Listen
824	The Development Of Man
829	The Essence Of Torah
1200	The Gift Of Torah
1201	My Share In Torah
1395	Preparation For Torah
1402	My Personal Torah
1765	What We Gained At Sinai
1768	The Bottom Line
1770	Am I Ready For Torah
1969	Kabalas Hatorah
1972	The Meaning Of Torah

THE THREE WEEKS AND TISHA B'AV

125	Mourn With Joy
127	Torah Never Went To Golus
566	The Golden Calf
569	Building The Bais Hamikdash With Our Fire
704	I, As A Walking Bais Hamikdash
708	Selfless Love
843	Let's Build The Third Bais Hamikdash
849	Make Use Of Your Intellect
855	Let's Represent G–D
858	Life As A Service To Hashem
859	Me, As A Torch Of Life
1019	Build Your Bais Hamikdash
1023	Turning Sadness Into Joy
1028	The Birthday Of Moshiach
1221	Today's Bais Hamikdash
1226	Rebuild The Bais Hamikdash
1228	True Value Vs. Symbolic Value
1233	You As A Bais Hamikdash
1226	Rebuild The Bais Hamikdash
1228	True Value Vs. Symbolic Value
1233	You As A Bais Hamikdash
1462	Let's Meet Hashem
1626	How To Build The Bais Hamikdash
1627	How To Prepare For Life
1628	The Birth Of Moshiach
1630	Have I Done My Share? (Tisha B'av)
1631	Shabbos Chazon — Nachamy Me As One
1749	

AUDIO TAPES
BY RABBI EZRIEL TAUBER

1790	Let's Build The Bais Hamikdash		1642	The Gift Of Rosh Hashono
1793	The Unity Of The Jews		1826	Make Yourself Ready
1794	The Birth Of Moshiach On Tisha B'av		1837	Preparing For Trial (Advanced)
1799	What Are We Missing?		1842	Questions And Answers
			1845	What Are We Giving To G–D?

ELUL

YOM KIPPUR

72	From The Depth I Call Out To You, Hashem		722	Take Yom Kippur With You
132	Mechanics Of Teshuva		881	Join Me Totally
135	A Real Chesed		883	Do It For Your Name
136	Teshuva With Simcha		1061	The Mitzvah In Teshuva
249	Teshuva With Shofar		1480	I Am Ready For Trial
250	New Times Of Teshuva		1482	Corronate Me
261	My Only Request Of Hashem		1483	Chesed, All The Time
338	The Value Of Time		1647	My Real Identity
446	Be An Original Jew		1650	Let's Thank Hashem
600	Meaning Of The Akaida		1846	Teshuva — Find Yourself
711	Fill In Your Time		1847	Connecting Yom Kippur And Succos
719	Obtaining Love Of Hashem			
720	Choose Life			
862	Truth			SUCCOS
864	In The Book Of Life		603	Decoration To G–D
872	Know G–D (Part A)		890	The Meaning Of Simcha
872	Our Crucial Days (Part B)		894	The Real Truth
1033	The Advantage Of Elul		1849	Let's Take Tishrei With Us
1039	The Concealed Power In You		1851	The Simcha Of Succos
1048	My Resolution			
1265	A Full Jew			CHANUKAH
1467	Only One Goal In Life		161	The Eternal Light
1470	What Is There For Us To Give?		271	Chanukah, 5745
1472	What Are We Giving To Hashem?		746	Bring Chanukah
			920	Why Are We Hated
1643	Elul		926	Me As Hashem's Candle
1824	How To Develop Simcha		935	Mitzvas Yediah — Emunah
1844	We Look For You		939	Me As A Chanukah-Light
			1295	The Four Golus
	ROSH HASHANAH		1306	Surprises About Chanukah
			1310	Bayomim Hohaim Bizman Hazeh
718	Two Ways Of Praying			
867	What Can I Give To Hashem?		1515	Chanuka
869	Let's Be Honest		1518	Self Esteem
876	Corronate Hashem		1690	Kindle Your Own Flame
878	Make Me King		1691	To Thank And To Praise
1034	Let's Corronate Hashem		1880	The Miracle Of Chanuka Today
1035	I, As A Representative Of Hashem		1884	Chanuka Today
1055	Power Of Prayer		1893	The Structure Of A Jew
1259	Please Corronate Me			

AUDIO TAPES
BY RABBI EZRIEL TAUBER

PURIM

105	How To Oppose Amalek And Pharaoh	
394	The Definition Of "Yehudi"	
777	Fight Amalek	
779	Develop Simcha	
784	Enjoying The Golus	
792	The Homon Of Today	
793	Mordechai And Esther Today	
971	How To Generate Simcha	
972	Assimilating Whilst Religious	
974	Pesach — Purim — Pesach	
1159	How Is Amalek Effecting Us	
1344	A Successful Simcha	
1359	Revelation Of Yisroel	
1377	Opportunities You Might Miss	
1557	Pharaoh-Amalek/Purim-Pesach	
1561	Getting Rid Of Amalek	
1562	The Final Of Amalek	
1719	How To Develop Simcha	
1720	Simcha Against Amalek	

SPECIAL SELECTION ALSO SUITABLE FOR BEGINNERS

75	Introductory Lecture To Non-Committed Jews	
93	Business And Torah	
146	For Beginners	
165-A	Creation And Its Purpose — A	
165-B	Creation And Its Purpose — B	
167	Business And Torah	
170	Life After Death	
176	Is There Everyday Life?	
201	Purpose Of Life (Part 1)	
202	Mysticism In Everyday Life (Part 2)	
203	Mysticism In Everyday Life (Part 3)	
241	Who Am I?	
250	New Times Of Teshuva	
269	Should We Isolate Or Integrate?	
295	Real Life	
307	Jewish Concept Of Woman	
316	The Structure Of The Jewish Nation	
317	To Appreciate Our Role	
323	Should We Plan?	
338	The Value Of Time	

354-A	Codes In The Torah — A	
354-B	Codes In The Torah — B	
394	The Definition Of "Yehudi"	
757-A	Creation And Its Purpose — A	
757-B	Creation And Its Purpose — B	
758-A	The Definition Of A Jewish Nation — A	
758-B	The Benefit Of Suffering — B	
759-A	Torah Idea Of Marriage — A	
759-B	Torah Idea Of Marriage — B	
796	Be A Proud Jew	
817	Torah Idea Of Marriage — A	
817	Reliance On Effort — B	
818	The Value Of Life	
855	Let's Represent G–D	
872-A	Know G–D — Part A	
872-B	Our Crucial Days — Part B	
966-A	Codes In The Torah — A	
966-B	Codes In The Torah — B	
1003	The Meaning Of Happiness	
1101	Destiny Of Life	
1316	Appreciate Life	
1341-A	Codes In The Torah — A	
1341-B	Codes In The Torah — B	
1431	You Can Be A Prophet	
1452	Two Parts Of Life	
1455	Are We Chosen?	
1461	We, In Making Moshiach	
1467	Only One Goal In Life	
1489	To Live For Now	
1497	We — As Hashem's Ambassadors	
1502	A Life Which Is All Good	
1506	Yaakov Tricks Eisav, Why?	
1508	Yaakov Vs. Eisav	
1511	The Real Reason For Anti-Semitism	
1522	Questions And Answers	
1532	Torah As A Map	
1549	Mishpotim	
1581	Avrohom — Today	
1603	The Spies Of Today	
1668	The Foundation Of Life	
1671	Could A Holocaust Happen Without G–D?	
1731	How Judaism Developed	
1742	Men's Development	
1751	Three Steps In Belief	
1762	Respect Yourself	
1763	Reconciling The Physical And The Spiritual	
1768	The Bottom Line	

AUDIO TAPES
BY RABBI EZRIEL TAUBER

1774	The Value Of Life
1775	Prophecy Fulfillment In Our Days
1782	Understanding Suffering
1788	Build Your Temple
1793	The Unity Of The Jews
1799	What Are We Missing?
1802	Living Each Day
1845	What Are We Giving To G–D?
1852	Introduction To Torah
1867	Ask Questions
1869	The Tenth Test
1879	The Formation Of Man
1881	Philosophy Or Faith
1888	The Power Of Faith
1893	The Structure Of A Jew
1896	Nature Vs. Miracle
1901	The Secret Of A Jew
1905	Life After Life
1908	If You Choose Me Then I Choose You
1918	Building Self Esteem
1923	Love Your Fellow Man
1944	Our Duty Today
1958	A Quality Life
1963	Discover Yourself
1973	The Beauty Of Shabbos

TAPES SERIES
BY RABBI EZRIEL TAUBER

Parsha Series (70 tapes, more in progress). This series, starting with the first pasuk of Bereishis, proceeds sometimes verse by verse through each parsha. Sefer Bereishis is complete in tapes 1-39.

Chovos Halevavos (100 Tapes)
Chovos Halevavos — Bitachon (4 Tapes)
Maharal — Netzach Yisroel (53 Tapes)
Maharal — Ohr Chodosh (3 Tapes)
Maharal — N'siv Hateshuva (18 Tapes)
Maharal — Geviros Hashem (55 Tapes — More Upcoming)
Maharal — Rosh Hashono (3 Tapes)
Ramchal — Da'as Tvunos (73 Tapes)
Ramchal — Derech Hashem (7 Tapes)
Ramchal — Mesilas Yeshorim (62 Tapes)

Tefillah (4 Tapes)
Shir Hashirim (12 Tapes)
Koheles (29 Tapes)
Tanya (52 Tapes)
Series Of Tapes For Chassanim (5 Tapes)
Series Of Tapes For Kallahs — Various Speakers (6 Tapes)
Questions And Answers (4 Tapes)

NOW AVAILABLE

Set of 8 cassettes by Rabbi E. Tauber for Chassanim, and set of 8 cassettes by various speakers for Kallahs. Each comes in a beautiful Album *suitable for a gift* ($32.00 per set).
The book "Choose Life!" on 4 audio-cassettes in one convenient Album ($16.00).

GREAT GIFT IDEA!

You can also order any other set of tapes (make up your own combinations) packed in an Album. (Minimum of 8 tapes, no extra charge for the Album.)
In addition there are tapes from many Seminars in English, Yiddish and Hebrew (series of about 10-12 tapes), as well as tapes for Russian-speaking people. The tapes for Russians are in English with a translation into Russian.

TAPES AVAILABLE FOR VARIOUS SELF-HELP GROUPS

Series Of Lectures For Divorcees
Series Of Lectures For Childless Couples
Series Of Lectures For Single Girls
Series Of Lectures For Widows
Series Of Lectures For Bereaved Parents
Series Of Lectures For Second Marriages

All of the above mentioned tapes are suitable and very helpful for any other kind of problem or difficult situation you might find yourself in.

Video Tapes
By Rabbi Ezriel Tauber

VIDEO TAPES
RABBI EZRIEL TAUBER

1. The Definition Of Truth
2. Creation And It's Purpose
3. Definition Of Life
4. Torah Concept Of Marriage
5. Prophecies Materialized In Our Times
6. Codes In The Torah
7. "Golus" — The Benefit Of Suffering
8. Panel Discussion — Questions And Answers
9. Times Of Moshiach
10. Efforts And Bitachon Towards Parnassa (Making A Living)
11. Practicality In Day To Day Life
12. Soul Searching (With Brian Weiss, MD)
13. Choose Life
14. "We Are One" — Why And How
15. Us In Creation
16. Tranquillity In Business

BOOKS

In today's times of stress and spiritual alienation, everyone feels a void somewhere in his or her life. Whether beginner or advanced scholar, the books of Rabbi Ezriel Tauber have helped people fill their voids. A survivor of the Holocaust, Rabbi Tauber's method—backed by years as a teacher and counselor—emphasizes the importance of learning to help oneself. Marriage, finances, doubts—his books cover the gamut of life's experiences and help you become your own psychologist and spiritual guide.

Self Esteem

Self-Esteem is a treasure map to the self. More than a manual of ideas on feeling good about oneself, it is the personal account of four different adults (based on true case histories) whose difficulties in life have negated their feelings of self-worth, making them anxious and unhappy. **Self-Esteem** will give you both the inspiration to undertake that epic journey to the center of yourself, as well as the practical advice how to stay on course during the often stormy days and nights of that journey.

(284 Pages)

Choose Life!

Choose Life! is an impact book. David, a 30-year-old professional, found out he had cancer and was so depressed that he decided not to take the chemotherapy that could save him. Reading **Choose Life!** changed his entire outlook and he decided to undergo the therapy with renewed courage. **Choose Life!** delivers . . . Rabbi Tauber shows us how to find ultimate meaning in our lives. Whether for yourself or a friend, choosing **Choose Life!** is a choice you will not regret.

(238 Pages)

Beyond Survival

Beyond Survival is based on the famous Thirteen Principles of Maimonides. However, whereas most expound on the Thirteen Principles to teach the basic tenets of Jewish faith, Rabbi Tauber goes beyond that and shows how each principle is a vital tool for spiritual growth and personal development. For instance,

- belief in the Creator's oneness is the foundation of self-esteem
- understanding what it means to believe in the coming of the Messiah is the psychological cornerstone for conquering adversity
- knowing that your body will come back to life will revolutionize the way you think of your physical self and surroundings.

Understood properly, the Thirteen Principles will naturally produce a penetrating, soulful outlook on life which helps you deal with the most difficult and confusing situations you find yourself in—be they family relationships, raising children, making a living, surviving a crisis, etc. In some ways the most inclusive of Rabbi Tauber's books, **Beyond Survival** is sure to help you turn every life experience and difficulty into a self-replenishing wellspring of renewal and growth.

(177 Pages)

BOOKS BY RABBI EZRIEL TAUBER

Darkness Before Dawn

Darkness Before Dawn is a book about how to grow from adversity. Proceeding with the assumption that the community is simply a larger version of the individual, it discusses the reasons behind the long history of Jewish suffering. Ultimately, the tragedy of the Holocaust is discussed. The end result is a document which helps each of us grapple with and overcome the personal holocaust we may be suffering. As a survivor of the Holocaust, the book is central to Rabbi Tauber's entire outlook and includes some of his most personal, gripping, and profound words. No one is immune to the trials and tribulations of suffering. No one. Yet, the darkest part of the night is the moment just before dawn. Help yourself or someone you know learn to grow from hardship and tragedy.

(274 Pages)

I Shall Not Want

I Shall Not Want: The Torah Outlook on Working for a Living delves into the simple yet profound message of faith. At the same time, it endeavors to show how pursuit of career and financial gain need not be a contradiction to faith. Indeed, in the Jewish perspective, each potentially enhances the other. True inner peace should not be dependent upon economic peaks and valleys. *I Shall Not Want* can help you attain the peace of mind necessary to pass unscathed through your personal valley overshadowed by death.

(134 Pages)

To Become One

To Become One: *The Torah Outlook on Marriage* "should be required reading for a couple about to be married and for many that are already married," writes a major Jewish periodical. Drawn from over three decades of counseling experience, Rabbi Tauber presents the deep underpinnings of the most profound of human relationships and includes a plethora of practical strategies for side-stepping or resolving conflicts. His formula for successful marriage has helped marriages of all types, even ones that were unhappy for over twenty years! Whether you are happily married, unhappily married, or just thinking about marriage, this book supplies the basic tools that can help you become one with your spouse.

(180 Pages)

Days Are Coming

Days Are Coming is a fascinating dialogue between a rabbi, an atheistic Israeli Zionist, and a searching American collegiate. More than just good entertainment, it is designed to help you feel in greater control of the ominous and foreboding events happening in our days. We have no need to be reminded of the upheavals occurring all over the world. Some believe them to be heralds of a new age. Others are confused and fearful, and only see in them the ugly face of fanaticism. The Jewish world, too, has undergone major upheavals. Do they portend good or bad? Is there something we can do about it? Read ***Days Are Coming***.

(226 Pages)

Rabbi Ezriel Tauber, holocaust survivor, and a truly international speaker, not only lectures to audiences in all major U.S. cities from coast to coast, but also in such places as Jerusalem (and all over *Eretz Israel*), Montreal, Toronto, London, Brussels, Moscow, Johannesburg, and even Hong Kong and Bangkok. His books — adapted from only a few of his more than **3,000 recorded lectures** — have been translated into Hebrew, Spanish, French, German, and Russian.

TYPICAL TOPICS

- The pursuit of money
- Soul mates
- Marriage & Communication
- Life after death
- Finding tranquillity
- Spirituality
- Maintaining standards in corrupt surroundings
- *Bitachon, Chinuch, Tefillah, Yom Tov*
- And more . . .

Join Rabbi Tauber's tape membership club for a low one-time price and receive **24 inspiring, timely, tapes** (exclusively recorded for members) shipped twice a month for the next 12 months.

Call Shalheves to place an order or for a FREE CATALOG
1-800-998-0400